Contents

CAUGHT IN KUWAIT

Fern Gibson Babcock

CAUGHT IN KUWAIT

A story of God's miraculous care in modern times

Fern Gibson Babcock

Pacific Press Publishing Association
Boise, Idaho
Oshawa, Ontario, Canada

Designed by Dennis Ferree
Cover photo by AP/Wide World Photos
Typeset in 10/12 Century Schoolbook

In order to protect the characters, many of whom still re-
side in the Middle East, the author has changed many
names, locations, sex, and nationalities. The basic facts,
however, are true and are recounted for the glory of God.

Copyright © 1992 by
Pacific Press Publishing Association
Printed in United States of America
All Rights Reserved

Library of Congress Cataloging-in-Publication Data:
Babcock, Fern Gibson.
    Caught in Kuwait: a story of God's miraculous care in
modern times / Fern Gibson Babcock.
          p.   cm.
ISBN 0-8163-1087-4
    1. Enden, Mark. 2. Seventh-day Adventists—Kuwait—
Clergy—Biography. 3. Adventists—Kuwait—Clergy—Biog-
raphy. 4. Iraq—Kuwait Crisis, 1990-1991. I. Title.
BX6193.E52B33   1992
286.7'5367'09049—dc20   91-40983
                                                        CIP

92 93 94 95 96 • 5 4 3 2 1

Dedication

To Del and Mark, who had the courage to tell it like it was
To Mom, who never doubted me
To George, who hugged me through the hard parts
To David and Sherri, whose phone bills soared as they encouraged Mom
To Evelyn and Inza, who faithfully read and critiqued every page
And to all my Muslim friends, who so patiently explained their beliefs and culture—and won my heart

Chapter 1
Safe in Kuwait

"Have you lost your mind?" Del stood at the top of the stairs in her Kuwaiti apartment, staring in astonishment at the hundred-pound sacks her husband was hauling in from the car. "When you said you were going with Proshad to pick up a few groceries, I never dreamed you'd come home with half a ton of food! What am I supposed to do with two hundred pounds of rice? And hundred-pound sacks of— what is that?"

"Oatmeal, cornmeal, milk powder, and beans!" Mark announced proudly. "And the five-gallon cans are corn oil!"

"But there are only five in our family," Del protested. "I'm not running a restaurant!"

Mark dragged the last bag through the front door of the house and into the large first-floor room that served as a meeting place for the Indians, Pakistanis, British, and Filipinos who made up the Seventh-day Adventist congregation that he and Del were pastoring in Kuwait. He stood up, rubbing his back and grinning at his wife's reaction.

"Oh, I don't know," he teased. "I'm going to be gone two months. Maybe without me here to keep things lively, you'll be glad to start a restaurant! Seriously though, Proshad took me to this wholesale market, and I just couldn't resist

9

the prices. I got that hundred pounds of beans for what we usually pay for ten pounds in the store. I figured that even if we only used half of it, we'd save money. And we might share with some of the church members. Now help me figure out where to store this stuff."

Shaking her head, Del descended the stairs to help her husband.

"You are impossible, Mark Enden! I never know what you're going to do next!"

Her husband laughed. "Aren't you glad you won't have to bargain in the market while I'm traveling around the Gulf? I don't like your going down there by yourself. Here. Pull on the top of this bag while I push from the bottom!"

Four months earlier, Del, Mark, and their three boys had moved into the second floor of this residential building, which housed the Adventist church. Just a few weeks before, their goods had finally arrived from the States, and the contents of their shipment already crowded the apartment. The three preschoolers had welcomed their long-lost toys with shrieks of joy, while Del gratefully unpacked her cooking utensils. Mark was delighted to find that his seventy-five boxes of books had arrived safely but was annoyed to discover that they all had to pass censorship before being allowed to enter the country.

Every day that week he had gone down to the dock to sit with the inspectors as they leafed through book after book. At first very brusque and efficient, by the end of the second day of sorting and chatting, the censors had become more friendly. Still, they set aside about half the books for further investigation. Those volumes were still in the customs shed, a fact that worried the young pastor.

Mark valued very few things more than books. Experience was one of them. It was impossible for him to put a dollar value on his years as a doctor's child growing up in southern Asia, speaking the language, eating the food, and enjoying the challenge of living in a foreign country. The experience was priceless—and so exhilarating that when he had a chance to return to Pakistan as a volunteer during his college years, he quickly accepted the challenge of teaching English to Pakistani students.

During his stay in that country, the young man became fascinated with the culture. The Muslim religion had so much to be admired. Faithful Muslims prayed regularly each day, fasted during daylight hours for a month each year, gave generously to the poor, refused to touch pork or liquor of any kind, and encouraged strong family ties. During school vacations, Mark backpacked across India, talking to both Muslims and Hindus, appreciating their friendliness and differing points of view. He left Pakistan at the end of his one-year term determined to return someday.

Since that year as a volunteer teacher, he had married Del Jones, an attractive nurse, and fathered three sons—a fact that was sure to bring approval in a Muslim land where sons are viewed as favors from God. Then, while pastoring a church in Pennsylvania, Del and Mark had been asked to consider an assignment in the Middle East.

"What can I do over there?" Mark inquired. "Our denomination doesn't have churches there, does it?"

"Not exactly," was the response. "But hundreds of Pakistanis, Indians, Filipinos, and Africans are working in the Middle East, and some of them are Adventists. We'd like you to pastor the little congregation in Kuwait and locate and encourage the other informal groups of Adventists that have sprung up among the foreign population in the Gulf states. You've had experience working overseas, and you appreciate the Muslim culture. We think you might really fit in this spot."

Mark and Del really wanted to go, but they had signed a five-year lease on the house they were renting, so it looked impossible. Still, Mark called the realtor.

"Our church has asked us to take an assignment in

Kuwait," he explained. "Unfortunately, we have a five-year rental lease on the house. If we decide to go, what would be involved in breaking the lease?"

The realtor answered quickly. "No problem. I'll just try to find another renter, and you'll need to cover the rent till I get one. Shall I start looking?"

Less than three weeks later, the realtor had found new tenants. It all worked out so quickly that Mark and Del felt sure God wanted them in the Middle East.

Following three months of Arabic instruction and a month of overseas orientation, the family flew to England for a week at the Seventh-day Adventist Global Centre for Islamic Studies. There they met others who had lived and worked in Muslim countries, and Mark had a chance to compare experiences and discuss Islamic theology. From England they traveled to Jordan, where they spent several weeks practicing their Arabic and discussing with Adventist leaders plans for their Kuwait assignment.

With three active boys to care for, Del found it hard to concentrate on language study. She managed quite well, however, until three-year-old Eric tumbled off a twelve-foot wall and suffered a concussion. For the next few days, Del watched him closely. Much to her relief, he seemed perfectly normal.

"Every mother ought to take nursing," she thought. "It's a good thing I knew what to look for."

Because Mark's parents were then working at a hospital in Pakistan, the young couple and their boys flew to Karachi for the Christmas holidays. After the holiday, Mark left Del and the boys with his parents and flew to Kuwait. Before they could join Mark, he would need to establish residency in Kuwait, a procedure that usually takes at least three months.

On the day he arrived, however, the computer in the permit office was down, and Mark's application for residency had to be hand delivered to the man in charge. The official looked at the document, shrugged, and stamped his approval on the paper at once, reducing a three-month wait to one hour!

"Thank You, Lord," Mark prayed that night. "I wasn't looking forward to three months without Del and the boys."

Back in Pakistan, Del immediately applied for visas for herself and the children. To everyone's astonishment, the documents arrived in two weeks instead of the usual two months.

"The Lord is certainly preparing the way for you and Mark," Dr. Enden told Del. "I've worked in several different countries, and I know this sort of thing doesn't just happen. The Lord has His hand over you."

When they arrived in Kuwait and Del resumed language study, the Lord even provided someone to help her with the housework and the children. One of Mark's Kuwaiti friends had an Indian secretary named Proshad, who was willing to help Mark with driving and shopping and other errands. Mark thought that was a fine idea, and Proshad moved into the custodian's apartment off the church courtyard.

When Del arrived and needed help, Proshad suggested his cousin, Rani, for the job. At first she just looked after the children, but soon Rani took over the cooking and some of the housework as well. As Del struggled with her Arabic lessons, she thanked the Lord daily for Rani's assistance.

Shortly after the family arrived in Kuwait, Mark left for a quick survey of believers in the Gulf area. In one country he found a group of twenty Asian Adventists who were delighted to see the visiting pastor and urged him to return as soon as possible and stay a week or two. In each country he followed up old leads, inquiring about Sabbath keepers. In one little-known emirate, he found several believers and formed a company. In another, he discovered seventy members meeting in a private home. Thrilled to find faithful Adventists in such isolated places, he flew back to Kuwait,

promising to return in a few months to hold special meetings. Now he was about to make good on that promise by
taking a two-month tour of the Gulf states. But before leaving, he had to get food for Del and the boys.

By the time Mark reached the top of the stairs, six-year-
old Ryan was helping Del pull on the bag, and Eric, three,
was getting in the way.

"I've got it, Del," he panted. "Get the kids."

The young mother grabbed a child in each hand and
backed out of the way as Mark slid the heavy bag down the
hall toward the pantry.

That night, after the boys were asleep, Mark flopped
onto the bed beside his wife and grinned at her.

"What's so funny?" she demanded.

He laughed aloud. "I was just remembering the look on
your face when you saw all those sacks of food today. It was
priceless! Anyway, now you can cook your heart out. You
can't say I'm not a good provider!"

"Too good!" Del responded. "I've got enough food for an
army—and speaking of armies, I sure wish you weren't
going to be gone so long. I hate staying here alone. You
never know when things may break loose in the Middle
East."

Mark reached over to rumple her dark hair.

"Don't worry, Del. You're safe here. Proshad will run
errands, and Rani will help you with the kids. Really,
you're safer here than in most big cities in the States. The
crime rate's lower here! If I thought you and the kids were
in any danger, I wouldn't go off and leave you. And even
though Jordan has an occasional riot, and Israel and the
PLO are always at it, they're a long way from here. All's
calm in Kuwait. The Emir sees to that. So forget that sub-
ject and give your deliveryman a good-night kiss. You're a
lousy tipper, you know that?"

Del rolled out of reach, laughing when he caught her and
pulled her back. With his wife in his arms, he no longer

worried about war or armies or unrest. He dismissed them all with one final thought—of all the countries he'd been in recently, Kuwait certainly rated as the most safe and secure.

Chapter 2
Into the Gulf

Getting food supplies was only one of the many things Mark needed to do before he could start his trip. Arranging for visas and entry documents to the various countries took a great deal of time, and he spent hours preparing talks and materials to leave with the groups he contacted.

When he had entered Kuwait, he'd brought with him two large suitcases—a tan piece full of personal items and the other a heavy bag of videos, audio cassette tapes, felt pictures for storytelling, and health and family-life materials. Standing in the customs line, Mark watched in alarm as inspectors dug through the suitcases of the passengers ahead of him, questioning many items and confiscating some.

"Lord," he prayed silently, "these are Your materials. Do with them as You see fit. But if You want me to use them, You'll have to get them through customs!"

Trying to maintain an outward calm, Mark hoisted his luggage onto the low counter in front of the inspector and greeted him. The man scowled.

"Open!" he demanded, pointing at the tan suitcase.

Mark complied at once, unlocking the bag and opening it to display a pile of dirty clothing. He smiled apologetically.

17

"Sorry it's such a mess," he said. "I've been traveling and haven't been able to wash."

The inspector sniffed disdainfully. Then he seized his chalk and marked both cases.

"Go," he said, waving his hand. "Go!"

The young man slammed shut the suitcase and exited quickly with both pieces of luggage intact.

"Thank You, Lord," he breathed.

He had run into another problem with the videos, however, when he discovered that the VHS format did not fit Middle Eastern equipment. The Breath of Life videos would be usable only if they were converted to a different type of tape. But the Lord worked that out too. A friendly Hindu agreed to copy the tapes onto cassettes compatible with local recorders, and he charged only for the cost of the new tapes! Now Mark felt sure that God had plans for those videos!

At family worship the morning of Mark's departure, the Endens prayed for God's blessing on the trip and the precious lecture materials. Then Mark picked up baby Loren, wiped the cereal from his face, and gave him a big hug.

"Me too," demanded Eric, holding up his arms.

"Me too," echoed Ryan.

Mark laughed and pulled the other two boys into his arms.

"I sure love you guys," he said. "Be good for Mommy, OK?"

The children nodded solemnly.

"Doesn't look like there's room in that hug for me," Del said. "I'll have to start a new one." And with that, she stretched her arms as far as they would go around the whole group. Then she and Mark squeezed, and the boys shrieked with delight.

Untangling himself from the family hug, Mark picked up his luggage and headed downstairs, the older boys scampering ahead. Del followed with the baby on her hip. At the front door, Proshad waited with the car to drive him to the airport. Before stepping into the street, however, Mark stopped to give Del a final kiss. He knew better than to do it outside, where a public display of affection would be frowned upon.

"Keep your chin up," he told her. "I'll call when I can. And I'll be back as soon as possible, believe me!"

Del smiled. "I'll be OK," she said. "But do keep in touch. I'd like to know where you are, at least."

Del and the children stood on the doorsteps, waving until the car was out of sight. She herded them back inside, got the boys busy playing, and sat down to write to her mother. Two months is a long time, especially when you have three preschool boys. She knew she would need to keep herself busy.

Proshad drove the Mitsubishi skillfully through the busy streets of Kuwait City. In some ways, it was like any other cosmopolitan city. Mark still marveled at its modern buildings and well-engineered highways. Skyscrapers, parks, Hardee's, Pizza Hut, and Holiday Inn gave the city a familiar appearance. Elegant shops sold items from around the world, and limousines vied for curb space at the large malls. Businesspeople hurried from air-conditioned buildings to air-conditioned cars, only their flowing robes reminding the American that he wasn't in the States. The scorching heat was another reminder. During the middle of the day, temperatures soared to 130 degrees Fahrenheit, figures that ordinary home thermometers couldn't even record. Silently Mark thanked the Lord again for air conditioning.

At the airport he said farewell to Proshad, boarded his plane, and settled back for the short flight to his first stop.

Upon arrival, he proceeded through immigration as usual, moving smoothly until he reached the customs area. Remembering the videotapes in his luggage, Mark prayed again for the Lord's will to be done. But this time, the inspectors pulled out the tapes and began questioning him.

"They are educational materials," he said. "Some of the tapes are on healthful living and ways to stop smoking."

The officials looked skeptical. "Let's take a look at them," they suggested. "Come into the viewing room."

For the next three and a half hours, several inspectors listened to excerpts from the Breath of Life meetings. The first tape, mostly on health, had their approval. The second, discussing salvation, did not.

"We'll have to keep your tapes for further evaluation. You can have them back in two weeks." The man spoke firmly.

"But I only plan to be here ten days," Mark protested.

The inspector shrugged. "Then pick them up as you leave the country," he suggested and turned to help the next passenger in line.

"Well," Mark thought, "it's up to You, Lord. Maybe these tapes aren't the right tool for this country. If so, it's all right with me." So, signing the required forms, he left the films and carried his luggage to the nearest rental counter to pick up a car.

"You must be very careful on roads at the edge of the city," the clerk warned him. "The winds blow sand across the pavement, and you can easily get stuck in it—or lose the road completely. We have sandplows, though, that keep the highways fairly clear—kind of like the snowplows in your country. You'll be OK if you're just careful."

"I'll stay inside the city," Mark promised.

The clerk laughed. "OK, and one more thing—in our country, if you ever hit a camel, you are at fault even if the camel is asleep in the middle of the highway at night. So don't hit a camel unless you are very, very rich, because the fine for hitting one is US $200,000! Camels are more valuable than cars here, and millions of dollars are bet on the camel races. Here are your keys. Have a pleasant stay!"

Mark drove off, keeping a sharp lookout for camels. Two

hundred thousand dollars would make quite a hump!

After checking into a hotel, he began making phone calls and locating Adventists who had moved to that city from all over the world. Before long he had found seventy believers and made arrangements to help them study the book of Daniel.

The week he arrived, meetings moved from a member's home to the newly built Ecumenical Christian Church, a building used by many denominations. About ten non-Adventists attended along with the Adventists, and at the end of his meetings, one was baptized. Mark was delighted to be the first to use the baptistry. The studies so inspired the members that they decided to continue them in smaller groups at private homes throughout the city after the pastor was gone.

When Mark left, airport officials returned all thirty videotapes, a move that pleased him greatly until the next day—when he discovered that the tapes had all been carefully erased!

His next stop was a country of contrasts. In one area, monsoons, bananas, and rain forests reminded him of South American jungles. At the other end of the land, however, sand dunes and hot desert winds prevailed.

His contact here was an Asian physician who had regularly been sending his tithes and offerings to church headquarters, even though there was no official church or pastor in his area. When Mark phoned him, the doctor was overjoyed that a pastor had finally come to visit.

"It has been years since we've had a pastor visit us," he exclaimed. "This is wonderful! Can you hold a meeting at my house tomorrow night?"

"Be glad to," Mark replied. "Is eight o'clock all right? I know your evening meals are usually later than ours in America."

"You're right," the physician agreed. "Why don't you come about seven and eat with us. We may not get started with the meeting, though, until about nine."

The next evening Mark made his way to the doctor's house, expecting to find a handful of believers. To his amazement, he found the room packed with Indian and Filipino business and professional people, only half of them Adventists. A non-Adventist Christian physician had come out of curiosity. He had always thought that Seventh-day Adventists did not really have a Bible-based religion, but the lively Bible study Mark held that night convinced him otherwise.

"Can we meet again tomorrow evening?" the group asked.

Mark agreed and evening after evening continued his Bible studies with the eager students.

One man had an especially thrilling story to tell. His grandparents had been Christians, but only recently had he decided to profess Christianity too. As a result of his decision, he had lost his job as a science teacher and was even committed to a mental institution for several months. His employer and friends thought he was losing his mind.

Free at last, he had no job and had stopped by an old Christian church to pray in the middle of the day. There in the cool dimness of the lobby, an open Bible on the table caught his attention. Stepping closer, he began reading the Ten Commandments for the first time. He was startled to find his name in the fourth commandment—Sabah, meaning seven. Pondering the significance of this, he turned to leave, but as he did so, he spotted a small notice on the bulletin board.

"Are you seeking truth? Come study the Bible with us."

Mr. Sabah took the scrap of paper from the board and put it in his pocket. That night, he turned up at the physician's house and joined the study group. When he learned that they were Seventh-day Adventists who kept the *seventh* day holy, he found that significant. Surely the Lord was speaking to him, calling him by name. He felt there was surely a message for him at these meetings.

The study series ended with a communion service. Forty believers participated and told of other Adventists scattered throughout the country. Mark wrote down names and addresses as fast as he could. The list totaled over one hundred in the capital city alone and seventy-five more scattered throughout the south. He could hardly believe it!

When he called Del that night, his exhilaration was evident.

"It's just like in Bible times," Mark told her. "Remember when Elijah thought there were no believers left except him? And God informed him that there were still seven thousand faithful ones that the prophet knew nothing about? Well, that's how I feel today. I knew we had a few believers here, but I had no idea there were nearly two hundred in this one little country. I guess my faith has been too small. God has been at work in people's lives even though there has been no organized church. It's really thrilling!"

"Yes, it is," Del agreed. "Things are happening here, too, Mark. You know the little Bible-study group you and the British woman, Luisa, were holding? Well, she called to tell me they needed more materials to keep them going till you get back. What do you suggest I give her?"

Mark thought a minute.

"Everyone's really enjoyed the studies we've been having here," he said. "Why don't I fax my materials to Luisa's office? That ought to hold her till I get back."

When he hung up, Mark rode the elevator down to the hotel lobby and faxed Luisa twenty pages of Bible-study outlines. Weeks later he discovered that he'd used the wrong fax number, and the material had never reached Luisa's office. He laughed, imagining some businessperson being deluged with page after page of Bible-study materials.

"God moves in mysterious ways," he told Del when he

heard about the misrouted faxes. "In the kingdom, we may find out that someone studied those fax pages."

At his next stop Mark found eighteen believers who met regularly. Twice they gathered in his hotel room to study and pray together. This stop was especially difficult for Mark because the Muslim fast of Ramadan began while he was there.

All around the world, faithful Muslims fast throughout the month of Ramadan. No water or food passes their lips during daylight hours. In many countries, motorists eating snacks or candy are stopped and warned that such activity is forbidden. Some Western-style hotels, however, offer discreet room service for their non-Muslim guests. Mark kept crackers and dried fruit in his room, and if he ate or drank during daylight hours, he did it behind a locked door.

The fast seemed hardest on construction workers, who toiled in the hot sun all day without water. For this reason, workdays were shortened and rest times extended.

At the end of the day, everyone waited anxiously for the announcement that the day's fast was over. In the marketplace a crier ran through the streets, ringing a bell to announce the end of the fast.

Business ground to a halt. Shopkeepers set out bottles of soda and plates of dates and nuts for themselves and their customers. All over the city, people rejoiced together at the breaking of the fast. Later in the evening, they went home to a feast, often eating until well after midnight.

By 4:00 a.m. the women were in the kitchen again, preparing a big predawn meal. As morning approached, the voice of the muezzin came over the loudspeakers mounted in the minarets of the mosque, warning the faithful that the fast was about to begin again. For the last half-hour before daybreak, the muezzin intoned a countdown with commentary. As mothers hurried to give their children a final drink, he finally announced that the fast had begun.

Since the fast was kept so rigorously, even non-Muslims

often joined in the fast to avoid distressing those who wouldn't allow themselves to eat. Work hours were shortened, people took long afternoon naps, and foreigners visiting during Ramadan got little business done.

Between Ramadan and the summer heat, Mark found it difficult to locate missing members. Many of the Indians, Pakistanis, and Filipinos had gone to their own countries for vacations. Sweltering in the heat of the last day of July, he began to think they were more clever than he.

As he made his way back to the hotel that afternoon, Mark felt drained of energy and purpose. For six weeks he'd been traveling and working; suddenly he had an overwhelming desire to go home. Nothing was really scheduled. Nothing needed to be canceled. Del's birthday was coming up August 5. The more he thought about it, the more he felt he shouldn't leave her to celebrate her birthday alone in a foreign land. On the spur of the moment, Mark called his airline and found that there was space available on the last flight of the day. He changed his ticket at once.

Suddenly, the heat seemed bearable. Tonight he'd be back home! How surprised Del and the boys were going to be! He picked up the phone and placed a call to Kuwait.

His wife answered.

"Hey, Del. It's me. Your personal pastor! How're you doing?"

"Mark! Why are you calling in the middle of the day? Oh, it's good to hear from you. We're fine, but Loren's been so fussy. He's cutting three teeth at once, and it's awful. I'd love to give you these boys for a few hours."

"Well, maybe that can be arranged. Do you suppose you could work an airport pickup into your busy schedule tonight?"

"Oh, Mark, quit teasing. You know you've got two more weeks to go."

"I *did* have, but I'm cutting the trip short. Can you pick me up tonight at eleven-thirty?"

Her shriek nearly burst his eardrums.

"You're not kidding? Oh, honey, that's great. I'll be there for sure! Oh, dear!"

"What's wrong? Isn't the car working?"

Del laughed.

"No, it's fine. It's just that I had planned to surprise *you* when you got home. I reserved a room at the Messilah Beach Hotel to celebrate our anniversary and to be together again. You know how little privacy we have living right above the church. I thought it would be really great to relax around the pool, order meals, and forget about church problems for a while. But maybe I can make an earlier reservation. Let me check on it. Anyway, I'm sure glad you're coming home early. The boys will be wild! What airline are you on?"

"Kuwait Air, flight 740, at eleven-thirty-two. The hotel idea sounds wonderful! I could use a little family time. And I'll be delighted to watch the boys and let you suntan. See you tonight—and Del, I love you!"

Hanging up the phone, Mark hurriedly packed his bags and checked out of the hotel. At the airport he returned the rental car and checked in for his flight nearly two hours early! He wanted to make sure nothing delayed his departure.

It was nearly midnight when he emerged from the Kuwait City airport, struggling to hang onto luggage, Ryan, and Eric at the same time. When they reached the car, Del hugged him and handed him the baby.

"It's your turn to hold him, sweetie," she said. "I'll drive."

Several hours later the boys were finally in bed, and Mark and Del had time for themselves.

"You were so sweet to come home early and surprise us," Del said, snuggling into the curve of her husband's arm. "I dreaded being alone on my birthday, but I didn't want to say anything."

Mark wrapped the other arm around his wife and kissed her.

"My pleasure!" he said. "Sorry I spoiled your surprise, though."

"Oh, you didn't! I couldn't get the reservation changed at the Messilah Beach Hotel, so I got one tomorrow at Holiday Inn instead. It's not as close, but that's OK. We're booked for two nights. Now don't fuss! We haven't spent anything on ourselves lately. Think of this as an investment in family!"

Mark laughed.

"You're terrific, you know that, Del? And I'm not fussing. I'd go to a hotel with you anytime! Now turn out that light! Family time has officially begun!"

Chapter 3

A Birthday Surprise

On Wednesday morning, August 1, Mark's sleep was interrupted by the patter of running feet followed by a violent pounce on the bed.

He pulled his pillow over his head.

"Go away," he mumbled. "Go back to bed."

Ryan giggled and tugged at the pillow. "Daddy's under here," he told Eric. "Pull!"

As both little boys tugged at the pillow, Mark let go, tumbling them backward. Del woke to laughter and a father/sons wrestling match. She reached for Eric.

"Come here, Rick-Rick," she ordered, and pulled him down beside her, woofing his soft neck and tickling him. He shrieked with laughter.

When everyone paused for breath, Mark asked, "What shall we do today, fellows? Want to go to the park?"

"Carnival," Ryan suggested, his brown eyes dancing. "We can ride the Ferris wheel!"

"That's an idea. How about it, Mommy? Where shall we go?"

Del swung her feet out of bed and felt around for her slippers.

"Well, first we've got to get some breakfast and pack

29

suitcases. But after that—I don't care where we go as long as we wind up at the Holiday Inn by midafternoon. I'm looking forward to a nice swim in its pool."

Mark booted the boys out of bed and sat on the edge of it, stretching and yawning.

"Short night!" he commented. "By the time we get to the pool, I may want to snooze instead of swim! Anyway, run along, fellows, and get your clothes on. I'll be with you all day."

All the commotion awakened Loren, who was bouncing up and down in his crib, demanding to be let out. Del walked down the hall to his room, picked him up, changed his diaper, and carried him into the bathroom, where Mark was eyeing himself in the mirror. She plunked the baby down in the dry tub and pulled back the shower curtain.

"There you go, Lo-Lo! Watch Daddy shave! It's better than TV!"

And she went off to make breakfast.

It was midmorning by the time the family loaded their packed suitcases into the Mitsubishi, said goodbye to Proshad and Rani, and drove off for their mini-vacation. At the carnival park, the boys ran from one ride to the other, enjoying them all. Del and Mark took turns carrying Loren in the backpack and going on rides with the boys. Before long everyone was hot, thirsty, and hungry, so the family piled into the car and drove to the mall for drinks and French fries.

"Why don't you guys get some haircuts while we're here?" Del suggested. "We want to look sharp at our fancy hotel!"

"Shall we get Loren's hair cut too?" Mark teased, bouncing the baby so that his long blond curls bobbed up and down.

Del snatched the child from him.

"No way! You leave my baby's hair alone! It's beautiful!"

Mark laughed as he headed toward the barbershop,

holding Ryan and Eric by the hand.

About four o'clock, they checked into the Holiday Inn, changed into swimsuits, and jumped into the pool. During the rest of the evening they enjoyed the hotel recreation room, ordered a light supper, and watched TV. Del and Mark had worship with the boys and put them down for the night.

"I wish the kids would sleep in tomorrow," Del said wistfully. "Wouldn't it be great to sleep till nine?"

Mark laughed softly.

"Not a chance. They're early birds, and you know it. We had a good day today, though, didn't we, honey? We ought to make time for the family more often. Did you see Eric's eyes when he rode the little plane at the carnival? He was so excited. Seems like just yesterday we were toting *him* around in the backpack. These boys will be grown up and gone before we know it. But right now we'd better get some sleep while we can."

Mark was right. The boys were up bright and early—five o'clock, to be exact. Crawling out of their bed, they made their way to the TV set and pulled the ON button. Mark tried to ignore the sound, but some newscaster's insistent voice kept battering his sleep-fogged mind. Suddenly, one sentence fragment came through loud and clear.

". . . and battalions of Iraqi soldiers are pouring into Kuwait City."

He sat upright in bed, trying to focus his eyes and his mind on the screen.

"Del! Del! Wake up! Iraq has invaded Kuwait!"

Del opened her eyes and sat up too. Alarmed by the tone of their father's voice, the boys sidled toward the bed with frightened faces.

Bounding out of bed, Mark yanked back the drapes and stared down at the highway eight stories below. Trucks, tanks, and marching soldiers filled the road and spilled onto its graveled shoulders. Del came to stand beside him,

Loren on her hip.

"Can you believe it?" she asked incredulously. "Where are they all headed?"

"To Saudi Arabia, from the looks of it." Mark shook his head. "That's where this road goes. Isn't this weird? Because this hotel is close to the airport, it's so soundproof we can't hear a thing. It's like watching TV with the sound off. It doesn't seem real at all. Oh, look! There's smoke coming from the airport. I wonder if they bombed it."

"What's wrong, Daddy?" Ryan asked anxiously, tugging at his father's hand. "Are the soldiers going to shoot us?"

Mark dropped the drape, sat down in a chair, and pulled Ryan onto his lap.

"No, Ryan. It looks like the Iraqi army has come to take over Kuwait. We don't know why. We don't know what's happening. But we're safe here in the hotel. When the embassy opens, we'll call and ask them what to do. For now, you kids just play with your toys, and Mommy and I will listen to the news and see if we can find out anything more."

For the rest of the morning, Del and Mark stayed close to the TV set, watching news being made. Realizing that international phone lines might soon be cut, they began trying to get a call through to Del's parents in Pennsylvania. After four hours, Mark finally got the Joneses on the line and let Del talk to them for a few minutes to assure her parents they were safe and would try to keep in touch.

"Don't worry if you don't hear, Mom," she urged, "because the phone lines will probably be cut. We'll try to get messages to you any way that we can, but for now, we're safe in the Holiday Inn."

Del's parents were certainly thankful for that phone call, because it was a month before they had any direct word from their daughter again. And Del was right about the phone lines. They were cut that night. Later, Mark heard that a local technician had been ordered to cut them earlier and pretended to do so but didn't cut completely through the cable. This gave foreigners another twelve hours to contact their loved ones.

"I need to let headquarters know what's happening," Mark said and began dialing the headquarters for the Seventh-day Adventist Church in the Middle East. After many tries, he finally reached them with the message that they were safe.

When the boys began fussing for food, the Endens ordered breakfast in the room. Then the phone rang. It was Luisa Lane, a British Adventist who worked in Kuwait. A close friend of the Endens, she knew of Del's plan to surprise her husband with the hotel stay, so she knew where to find them.

"Good morning!" she said. "Or maybe it's bad morning. Have you seen the news?"

Del leaned close to the phone at Mark's ear so they could both hear. Mark spoke. "We sure have. The kids were up at five and turned on the TV. We've been watching it ever since. We've called Del's folks and church headquarters to let them know we are OK. What's going on over there?"

Luisa's voice tightened. "The streets are full of tanks and soldiers," she reported, "and I can hear explosions and gunfire. Mark, I'm scared! My apartment is right in the middle of things. What should I do?"

Del spoke up. "You can come here to us, Luisa, or you can go to the church and stay in our apartment. Rani and Proshad are there."

"Maybe I'll call Shireen to see if I can stay with her," Luisa said. "She's closer, and I might be able to get there if the streets clear a little. Keep in touch with me by phone, if you can. This whole thing's scary!"

A call to the American embassy shed little light on the situation. They confirmed the invasion of Kuwait but didn't know what to advise other than to keep a low profile and check back later.

After noon, Mark went down to the lobby and talked with the clerks. They seemed calm. The road in front of the hotel was now clear of military, so Mark decided to try driving back to the house to check on Rani and Proshad. Del wasn't keen on that idea, but her husband insisted.

"Oh, all right," she sighed. "You won't be happy till you do. Go ahead. But please be careful, honey. Don't take any chances. I don't want to raise these three boys alone!"

Mark laughed.

"Is that all I'm good for? Helping you raise kids? Anyway, I'll be careful. Be back soon."

An hour later, tired of trying to amuse the children in the room, Del called the desk clerk, who assured them it was perfectly safe to use the hotel pool. Relieved, she put on their swimsuits and took the boys down for a dip. They played happily in the wading pool, coming out to eat the sandwiches a waiter delivered to them.

Suddenly the roar of helicopters and airplanes broke the calm. Swimmers scrambled out of the water and ran under the patio overhang. Del stood there, trying to hold onto all three boys at once, wishing Mark were with her. What if they bombed the hotel?

As the sound of the motors receded into the distance, some of the swimmers ventured back into the water. Del let the boys play a few minutes more and then decided to return to the room.

Mark came back early in the evening with news of the outside world.

"I didn't have any trouble getting home," he reported. "I saw clusters of troops along the road, but when they stopped me, all they wanted was to know if I had any water. I didn't. I heard the Iraqis were attacking the Resistance forces near here today. They sealed off the block around the corner from here, and the Safeway store is bombed out now. It was so close, I was worried about you and the boys. Was everything all right here?"

Del brushed back her dark hair and sighed. "We didn't get hit, if that's what you mean. But we got out of the pool in a hurry when the helicopters came! All this uncertainty is nerve-racking. Did you find Rani and Proshad?"

"Yes, they were hiding in our apartment, watching the Iraqi news on TV. They seemed to be all right and had enough food. So I let them know we were OK, picked up a few toys for the kids, and came back the long way. Have you heard from Luisa?"

Del nodded. "Yes, she called. She made it safely to Shireen's house, and she's staying inside. She sounded a lot calmer. She tried to call England but thinks that all the overseas lines are down now."

"She's probably right. I'm glad we got through before they cut them. It's a good thing she moved. The streets are crawling with military personnel. She picked the safest place, I think. I'm glad she didn't decide to come here. Seems to me this room's getting more crowded all the time!"

The next day the hotel manager announced that the pool had been closed. Del had food delivered to the room twice that day, but it seemed to her that the second meal had rather small portions.

"Do you suppose they're trying to conserve food?" she asked her husband as she eyed her plate.

"I wouldn't be surprised," he replied. "Maybe we'd better get some crackers or something for the kids."

When the family rode the elevator down to the hotel shops on the ground level and bought a few food items, the shelves already looked rather bare.

That evening as the Sabbath began, they sang familiar Sabbath School songs and talked about angels and their protecting care. As far as they could tell, they were safe.

"If the UN steps in, this whole thing may be over in a week or two," Mark speculated. "If things don't get any worse, we might want to move back home and just hide out there. At least the kids would have more room to play."

"Let's see what happens," Del suggested. "I'm for going home if we can. My surprise hotel stay is turning out to be more of a surprise than I bargained for!"

Chapter 4
Escape to Home

Saturday morning Mark drove around, trying to assess the situation. When he encountered soldiers blocking the road, he started a conversation in Arabic. Their friendliness encouraged him to ask questions.

"Why is Iraq taking over Kuwait?" he asked. "This was so sudden."

The soldiers nodded.

"For us too," one confessed. "The operation was highly secret. Our officers knew what was happening, but we were just following marching orders."

"It was rumored that we were going to do joint maneuvers with the Kuwaiti troops," another told him. "I didn't know we were taking over Kuwait until we got here."

"Well, there's obviously an invasion," Mark said. "What do you think is going to happen next?"

A young Iraqi soldier shook his head. "I don't know. I just know our job is to man this checkpoint."

Mark sighed.

"Well, you're certainly stopping traffic! May I go now?"

"Sure, American. Go ahead. But you really ought to stay off the streets. You never know what might happen out here. If shooting starts, you might get hurt."

Mark thanked them and pulled away. Still, he wasn't quite ready to go back to the hotel. It was about time for Sabbath School, and he wanted to see if any members had risked coming to the church.

On the direct route, he was stopped again by a different military group and ordered to turn back. He turned around, drove until he was out of sight, and then doubled back on a different road, finally reaching the church. There he found some Indians and Filipinos looking anxious and worried.

"We were vacationing at the Holiday Inn when this started," he told them frankly. "Because I'm thinking of bringing the family home soon, I'd appreciate it if we didn't call attention to this place by holding meetings here for the next few weeks. It's dangerous for you to come here, and it's dangerous for us to have you here. Maybe you can come three or four at a time as if you are visiting. That wouldn't attract attention. Anyway, since we're all here now, let's have a season of prayer for our safety and for this country."

After the members left, Mark hunted up the Lego set for the boys and picked up clean clothes for all of them before cautiously returning to the hotel.

Sunday morning Del had to make several changes in the breakfast order because the kitchen had run out of some items.

"Why didn't you tell them it was your birthday and that they ought to go *find* the orange juice for you?" Mark joked. "I planned to be here to celebrate with you but not locked in a hotel room with three kids! What do you want to do for your birthday?"

Del laughed. "I want to go to the beauty parlor to get my hair cut," she said. "It's getting so long I can hardly stand it."

Mark whipped out his wallet and handed her a large Kuwaiti bill. "Here you go," he said. "Happy birthday. Get your hair cut and set and anything else you want. I'll take care of the kids this morning."

"That's a terrific present," she said. "Time for myself! I should have birthdays more often!"

Before breakfast arrived, the phone rang. It was Luisa.

"Happy birthday, Del. Are you all OK?" Her voice sounded worried. "Have you heard what's happening at the Messilah Beach Hotel?"

"No. What?" Del asked.

"The Iraqis have taken it over to house their officers. The Western guests are being rounded up and sent to Baghdad. Nobody knows why. I'm so glad you're at the Holiday Inn. I hear it's being left alone because the owner is an Iraqi."

Del and Mark exchanged glances.

"I'm glad we're here too, Luisa," Del agreed. "I was so upset that Messilah Beach Hotel couldn't change our reservation. Now it looks like the Lord had a hand in it, doesn't it? We're glad you're OK. We've been thinking of moving back to the apartment. Tomorrow we'll scout around and see how things are."

"Keep in touch," Luisa said. "I don't know how long I can stay here. I may need to move in with you yet."

"We'll let you know what we decide to do," Del assured her. "The embassy keeps saying we should just keep a low profile. I wonder whether we ought to try driving to the Saudi border to get out of this mess."

Mark interrupted.

"We'd be sure to get into trouble there, Del. The border's bristling with troops."

Del shrugged. "Did you hear that?" she asked Luisa. "Mark thinks we'd just run into all the border troops. Oh, well, we'll call. And thanks for remembering my birthday. My present from Mark is getting my hair done at the hotel beauty parlor. See you later!"

All morning Mark played with the children, sometimes taking them out into the long hall to run. Fortunately, guests were few, and the floor seemed rather empty. When the boys wearied of that activity, he herded them all into the fancy glass elevator and let them ride up and down the twelve floors, watching the cars in the parking lot grow smaller and larger as they went.

When Del returned, she was carrying a big white box.

"What's in there, Mommy?" Eric demanded. "What's in the box?"

Del set the container on the dresser and lifted the lid. Everyone peered inside at a tasty-looking Black Forest cake.

"There were two cakes left in the pastry shop," she told them, "so I bought one of them for my birthday. Why don't you order lunch, Mark, and we'll have cake for dessert!"

The cake made the occasion festive, although they soon discovered it was dry and not as tasty as it looked. Still, Del was glad she'd bought it. It made the day more special.

"Why don't you put the baby down for a nap and then snooze or read," Mark suggested. "I'll take Eric and Ryan down to the recreation room and teach them how to bowl. Maybe we'll even play a game of Nintendo."

Del laughed. "Who's being entertained?" she teased. "The boys are a little young for Nintendo, don't you think?"

"Oh, all right," Mark conceded. "I intend to play Nintendo myself! But anyway, I'll get the boys out of here for a while so you can have some peace and quiet. Happy birthday, Tweety!"

Monday morning the family decided to leave the hotel and drive past the apartment, just to check on things. They took no luggage with them, as they didn't want to alarm the security guards who were now stationed at the hotel entrance.

Driving through the city, they stared at the large shell holes in some buildings. It seemed unreal because they had heard no bombing or rockets in their soundproof hotel room. The stench of burning tires hung in the air. Although they passed many groups of soldiers, none made any move to stop them. Not far from the apartment, they discovered

Iraqi tanks. Nearby, soldiers were digging trenches. The Endens drove past a military post and turned into their own street, stopping in front of the apartment. After Mark checked it out, he signaled them to come inside.

Glad to be back in familiar territory, the boys raced around the church room and up the stairs, shouting for Rani. She welcomed them home and was sorry to hear they were just visiting.

"We may come back this afternoon," Mark told her. "I think we'd be safer here than in the hotel. I saw some Iraqi military checking in at the registration desk today. After what happened at Messilah Beach, I think I'd rather be home."

Back at the hotel, Del packed their bags. Mark carried them to the lobby, with his wife and the boys following him. At the front door the guards stopped them.

"Better you stay here, sir," they said politely. "No go outside. Very bad."

Mark turned around and headed back to the elevator, the family still trailing behind. On the way up, Del spoke.

"Do you suppose they stopped us for our own safety? Or do you think we're being kept here?"

Mark shook his head. "It's anyone's guess. With the Iraqi officers checking in, I don't like not being allowed to leave. We can't afford to stay at this hotel much longer—and there's hardly anything left on the menu anyway! At least we've got food at home. Let's try again tomorrow but be a little more careful."

That night the American embassy approved the family's return to their apartment. The ambassador had made plans to evacuate them, along with several other families, but those plans had fallen through. After worship, Del tucked the boys into the hotel bed for what she hoped was the last time.

The next morning, she packed again. During family worship, Mark and Del both prayed for God's special protection that day. Then Mark wandered casually downstairs and paid their hotel bill. Afterward, he returned and helped Del strap Loren into the backpack and load the luggage onto the elevator. When they reached the first floor, Mark got off and walked straight out the door to the parking lot.

Del took the elevator back up to second and held it there, watching the parking lot through the glass until she spotted their Mitsubishi pulling up at the front door. Quickly she brought the elevator down again, and when it opened at the lobby, she grabbed the suitcases and the boys and walked straight out the door, looking neither left nor right as she pushed the boys and the luggage into the car. Hardly had her door closed before Mark was pulling away from the hotel. No one spoke for several minutes. When they turned onto a familiar side street, Del realized she'd been holding her breath.

As they passed Iraqi checkpoints, Mark either looked straight ahead or waved and kept on going. Before long they were in front of the apartment building, and Proshad and Rani were helping them move back in.

Since the boys seemed nervous about staying in their room alone, Mark dragged the double mattress back to the boys' bedroom. Their room at the back of the house appeared safer than the master bedroom, which faced the street. Loren seemed relieved to be back in his crib again, and Rani slept in his room to keep him company.

That night the family held a special thanksgiving worship, grateful that they were safely home again. Later, as Del padded barefoot past the pantry to get a drink of water, she stopped to stare at the big hundred-pound bags of food with new appreciation. If God cared enough to plan that far in advance for their food supply, surely He would see them safely through this crisis.

Chapter 5
Kuwaiti Hideout

The day after the Endens moved back home, Saddam Hussein announced that his country had officially annexed Kuwait and that it was now part of Iraq. The following day the borders of the country were closed, leaving about 3,000 Americans and thousands of other foreigners stranded in Kuwait. Mark was thankful they were not still living at the hotel, where their presence would be obvious.

Announcements on the local radio ordered all Westerners to report to certain hotels, bringing their food supplies with them. Some complied, but others, like the Endens, chose to ignore the order on the advice of their embassies.

During the first two weeks after the invasion, convoys of trucks loaded with food drove steadily north on the highway to Iraq. The three-year supply of staples that Kuwait had stocked in its port city was now on its way to Baghdad. Since the church was close to a highway, and Iraqi soldiers were quartered in nearby buildings, Mark covered the apartment windows with paper so that neither their movements nor lights would attract attention. He and Del discussed sleeping under the stairs and then dismissed the idea. They didn't want to seem paranoid.

The apartment was not in an ideal location. The nearby Kuwaiti Central Intelligence building was bombed and gutted. Not far away, a Kuwaiti man had stood by a barrel, watching an approaching Iraqi convoy. Suddenly he flipped the barrel on its side and rolled it directly in front of the oncoming tanks, where it exploded in a ball of fire, killing him and forty others in the blast. Many Kuwaitis felt so strongly about the invasion that they deliberately gave their lives in attempts to thwart it.

Anyone coming to the apartment had to pass an Iraqi tank dug into the ground in an open field, its guns ready to fire. The suburb also had a checkpoint with cannon and armed guards to control traffic to that part of the city.

The whole situation was strange. After most of the troops moved out of town toward the Saudi border, the citizens resumed their shopping and driving. When the fighting resumed, everyone stayed indoors. Because they were obviously Westerners, the Endens stayed inside most of the time, but that first week, Mark made a few trips to the American embassy when he couldn't reach it by phone.

Whenever Mark went out, he carried some money, his passport, and a thermos of water with him. He never knew what might happen before he could get back home. Carrying the water, however, was almost useless because whenever the checkpoint guards spotted the thermos, they helped themselves to nearly all the water.

Once, the guards asked him if he had water, and when he admitted that he did, they not only helped themselves to a drink, but kept the thermos and paper cups as well. Although they did so in a friendly manner, he decided it was the better part of wisdom not to argue over whose jug it was, lest they decide they liked his car too! The next day, Mark concluded it was getting too risky to go outside at all anymore.

Shortly after they arrived home, Luisa came to visit. Del and Mark welcomed her with hugs and hurried her upstairs to talk. Soon the phone rang, interrupting their conversation. It was Shireen, Luisa's friend, her voice strained and anxious.

"Luisa, after you left, some men came to our apartment to ask where you'd gone. You know your car had been parked on the street in front of the house. Well, they wanted to know where it was now and where you were. I don't think I'd come back here, if I were you."

After the call, Luisa discussed the situation with Mark and Del.

"You'd better stay here with us," Del suggested. "If they're watching you that closely, it's only a matter of time before they pick you up. The union's guest room on the second floor is empty. Want to stay there?"

Luisa agreed. Proshad moved her car to a more concealed spot, and the young British woman stayed.

A few days later, during a lull in the fighting, Luisa drove back to her apartment and retrieved her belongings and her ginger tabby cat, Bubble. A few years before, she had found him as a kitten under a city bridge, covered with sores and nearly dead. After she nursed him back to health, he became a real companion to her, and in this crisis, Luisa wanted her pet with her. She returned without incident, thankful that there was room at the church and that food was no problem.

As the Kuwaiti Resistance became better organized, two Iraqi checkpoints came under increasing nighttime attack. Located between them, the apartment was often caught in the crossfire. Ammunition ricocheted off the outside walls and occasionally came flying inside. To guard against stray bullets, Mark and Del pushed heavy wooden furniture and bookcases in front of the windows. Still, the gunfire at night made sleeping difficult.

To add to the misery, the air-conditioning unit in Luisa's room stopped working. She couldn't sleep in the heat and hauled her mattress downstairs to the church library, where it was cooler. She didn't like sleeping downstairs alone, but in the hot room upstairs, she wasn't sleeping at all.

A few nights later the family was awakened by sounds of activity in the courtyard of the house next door. Daylight revealed piles of Kuwaiti army clothing and guns. Mark and Proshad decided it was probably gear from the Resistance troops, items that were being hidden as the Kuwaiti soldiers adopted civilian disguise. Such close military activity alarmed them.

Mark and Del decided to move to the first floor, too, and sleep in the church meeting hall. Since it had several rooms surrounding it, the sanctuary appeared to be the safest and quietest spot in the building. Everyone pitched in to stack the folding chairs in one corner of the large room and haul the mattresses down from second floor. Before long, the church had become a giant bedroom, to the boys' delight.

Now that they had a food supply and a safe place to sleep, Mark began to be concerned over their water supply, which came from a large tank on the roof. Under normal circumstances, water trucks came by every two weeks and refilled the tank. Would that service continue now? Proshad contacted their water carrier, a friendly Palestinian. He agreed to continue water deliveries as long as they paid in cash. That was no problem at the moment, but no one knew how long the cash supply would hold out.

Still pondering the water situation, Mark's thoughts wandered to the courtyard. The baptistry was out there, a small above-ground tank! Why hadn't he thought of that before?

"Del, I think I'll fill the baptistry with water. Then if the water truck doesn't come, we'll have enough to manage for a while."

Del nodded agreement. "Good idea. Keep the kids out of it, though, or we'll be drinking swimming-pool water!"

In the summer heat, water in the rooftop tank almost

boiled. Because they were trying to conserve the precious fluid, Del and Mark attempted to make every drop serve more than one purpose. On bath days, they filled the tub with water early in the day so that it would cool down enough to bathe in. Del bathed all three boys at once. She and Mark took baths in the same water afterward, rinsing off with a dipper of clean water at the end. Next, Del washed clothes in the bathwater. Then she rinsed the day's dirty dishes in the tub before washing them in clean water at the kitchen sink. Finally, the liquid was scooped into buckets and used to flush the toilet. By the time it ran down the drain, the water had received maximum use!

The fact that the electricity remained on during these turbulent days was a constant amazement to the group. In phone conversations with others in hiding, they learned that there had been quite a few electrical failures in other parts of the city; in fact, the invaders had dismantled two power plants and left parts of the town without electricity. And because water was pumped to rooftop tanks by electricity, those areas had no water either. But there weren't many blackouts in the area of the church. Power surges were frequent, but those happened in normal times too. With temperatures hovering around 130 degrees, Mark feared air-conditioning breakdowns almost as much as water shortages. But although the one unit did quit, the second air conditioner kept the rest of the house comfortable.

During the day the boys played in the big room and up and down the stairs. The Lego set kept them busy for hours while they arranged the tiny blocks into tanks, planes, and rockets. Mark went upstairs every hour to listen to the BBC on shortwave radio and Iraq's news broadcast on TV. Rani did most of the cooking, and they all trooped upstairs for meals.

The adults spent their time reading, studying the Bible together, practicing Arabic, talking on the phone, or playing games. Mark had purchased an Arabic Nintendo disk containing fifty games. He began playing and got the boys interested too. Ryan did quite well, but Eric was frustrated because he couldn't work the keypad as fast as his brother.

Del discovered one game called Bomber Man. She played it repeatedly, taking out her frustrations by aggressively "bombing" the targets that appeared on the computer screen. She became so obsessed with it that Mark and Luisa dreaded seeing her head for the computer. Then Del discovered a European game called Tetris, the object of which was to fit various geometric shapes together to fill up spaces. Playing intense computer games challenged her, helped pass the time, and reassured her that she was using her mind.

Every three or four days Luisa and Mark would phone the British and American embassies to report in. Long before the invasion, the British embassy had divided the city into sections and appointed a British citizen as warden for each section. The warden's duty was to check on the welfare of all British citizens within his or her sector and report daily to the embassy. In this way, the embassy could destroy all lists recording names and addresses of British citizens and still keep track of the people through the wardens.

Back in Britain, a close relative of each Britisher in Kuwait received a daily phone call giving the current status of the person in hiding. The system was so efficient that once, when a warden called the embassy to report that eight Britishers had been captured and taken away, the information was on the BBC news within an hour! Luisa's mother was not only informed that her daughter was safe but also that she had received a monthly injection which her health required.

When Luisa became restless, Del found some needlepoint supplies and helped her begin a craft project. When Rani got bored, Del found her a crochet hook and thread. This occupied the young women for several days—until baby

Loren found Rani's crochet bag and scattered its contents. What he did with the crochet hook, no one ever found out. A thorough search of the building revealed nothing—and Rani was idle and bored again.

"We need another crochet hook, Mark," Del announced. "Luisa and I think we know where to find one in the mall. We haven't been out for weeks, and we're going stir crazy. Would you watch the kids while we go shopping?"

Mark looked up in alarm.

"Are you nuts?" he exploded. "Why risk your life for a crochet hook? What if you get captured?"

Del shrugged. "I know it's crazy—but I'm going to be really insane if I don't get away from here for a while. We'll take our car and be very careful. Things have been quiet for several days now, and others we talk to on the phone say they've been out and back safely. The military isn't after women, anyway. We're not in as much danger as you'd be."

Mark sighed and held up his hands in resignation.

"OK, OK, go ahead. In the midst of a war, you women still have to go shopping! Be very careful—and hurry back."

During the afternoon heat, when most of the city's residents were resting, Del and Luisa drove cautiously down the street and around the corner past the checkpoint. In a short time they were in the mall, exclaiming in disappointment over the lack of merchandise on the shelves and eyeing some Iraqi families who were shopping too.

Unfortunately, they didn't find a crochet hook, so they began their return trip. Out of curiosity, they decided to drive past the palace, where, according to news broadcasts, there had been a massacre. The route led past bombed buildings and burned tanks, but the palace itself saddened them most. The exquisite royal building lay in ruins, plundered and burned; and the bloodstains on the street in front shocked them with the peril they faced. The women drove straight home, resolving to stay in hiding until they could leave the country.

Proshad was in less danger than the Westerners, so every few days he would go to the market for fresh food. Once, when he had been gone all morning, everyone began watching for his return, worried that he might be having trouble.

"Is everything OK, Proshad?" Mark asked as he came in.

"Yes, sir. All OK."

"What did you get?" Luisa eyed his bag. "Is there still food in the market?"

Proshad began emptying his shopping bag onto the table.

"Fresh pita bread!" he announced. "I bought all they'd sell me—twenty-five loaves. But the line was so long, I had to wait five hours!"

"Thanks for being so patient," Mark said. "I love pita bread. I see you got some onions too. Say, Rani, how about lentil stew and pita bread for lunch?"

Another market trip nearly proved disastrous. Proshad entered a small grocery where Westerners frequently shopped and asked the clerk for peanut butter. Several Iraqi soldiers, casually helping themselves to the merchandise (much to the distress of the shopkeeper, who knew he'd never get paid for the items), overheard his request and confronted him.

"Why are you asking for peanut butter?" the soldiers inquired suspiciously. "That's an American food!"

Proshad thought fast. "Americans aren't the only ones who like peanut butter," he protested. "I learned to like it in India. You like peanuts, don't you? Peanut butter's just ground peanuts. It's good. You ought to try it."

The soldiers muttered among themselves, apparently trying to decide whether to follow this fellow to make sure he wasn't hiding Americans. Then one of them yawned.

"It's too hot outside," he said. "He's probably right. I know some Indians in Baghdad who like peanut butter."

Proshad paid for his groceries and strolled casually out of the store. But he took a winding route home, checking continually to make sure no one was following him.

The second Sabbath of the occupation, Del and Luisa held Sabbath School for the children. The familiar songs, finger plays, and stories seemed to calm both young and old. A few of the church members arrived quietly in small groups so as not to attract attention. Mark led them in a lesson study and prayer session while Del entertained the children with Bible stories illustrated with felt characters. The believers departed at various times, some leaving a gift of food for their pastor.

Under the circumstances, taking up a collection was hardly practical because Mark already had more Kuwaiti cash than he wanted. Just before the invasion, the congregation had given a special offering—entirely in Kuwaiti currency—for a radio tower in Italy. Before the treasurer could deposit the money, the invasion began, and banks were closed. He brought the offering and the account books to Mark one afternoon, telling him that he and his family were planning to leave the country if at all possible. Mark hid the funds in a briefcase, wondering what to do with them.

The value of the Kuwaiti dinar had changed overnight. Before the invasion, one Kuwaiti dinar equalled fifteen Iraqi dinars. After the invasion, Kuwaiti currency was declared illegal and was to be exchanged for Iraqi dinars on a one-for-one basis. On the black market, however, one could still get twenty Iraqi dinars for one Kuwaiti! Mark believed that the currency would stabilize in time. Meanwhile, he didn't want a stock of Iraqi dinars, so he resolved not to use the offering unless absolutely necessary but to save it until it could be of value to the denomination again.

The treasurer wasn't the only one fleeing. Many members of the little multinational church found ways to return to their homelands. Occasionally, one or two would stop by to visit the Endens, surreptitiously bringing them a delicious Filipino or Indian dish. Some came to say goodbye, others just to report what was happening to their friends.

"The DeRosas left last week," one member told Mark. "They paid someone to drive them to Baghdad and took only one suitcase apiece. I went by their house this morning and saw Iraqis coming out with their bedroom suite. I doubt they'll have anything left if they return."

"They may not have anything, period," Mark said grimly. "I heard yesterday that many of the foreigners who are fleeing through Baghdad have their luggage taken from them at the airport. I just pray they get out alive."

One Filipino family in particular seemed to be watching out for the Endens. Again and again they endangered their own lives to bring food and encouragement to their pastor and his family. Such selfless caring gave Mark and Del a real lift and made their confinement a little easier to bear.

Chapter 6

Free at Last

As the occupation continued, the Kuwaiti Resistance began to change its tactics. Direct confrontation was costing too many lives. For every Iraqi killed, the invaders would shoot from one to five Kuwaitis in retaliation. Because they prayed many times a day, wealthy Muslim families had erected small neighborhood mosques near their homes. At one of these, soldiers killed a large Kuwaiti family—inside the mosque at prayer. No one had dreamed that the Muslim invaders would desecrate a Muslim place of worship.

In the face of such attacks, the Resistance began to focus more on passive resistance and the concealment and care of foreigners hiding in their city. At the risk of their lives, Resistance members delivered diapers, medicines, bread, and fresh vegetables to those in hiding. They even arranged and paid for water deliveries.

From the beginning, adjusting to life in hiding was difficult for Mark and Del. Every morning for two hours, Rani would take the baby downstairs to play and leave Del upstairs with some time to herself. She started a piece of cross-stitch embroidery but found it hard to concentrate on the pattern. In fact, she found it hard to concentrate on anything. She spent hours pacing around the house rest-lessly or helping Rani cook. But even though they invented some very tasty dishes, Del had no appetite for them. In her quiet time alone, she studied her Bible and prayed for new ideas to keep herself and everyone else calm and occupied during their confinement.

The Endens' twelfth wedding anniversary came that week, and Del baked a cake to celebrate the event. Even that small variation in the day's activities seemed to ease tensions.

Mark seemed obsessed with the need to pack everything. Del refused to pack at all, reasoning that they were using their things right now, and if they did get out, their belongings probably wouldn't.

The most difficult days came after a routine had been established, and nothing of significance was happening. The interminable wait wore on everyone's nerves. Little mannerisms hardly noticed during normal times now became major irritations. They tried to remind themselves that close confinement requires extra patience but wound up snapping at each other anyway. Some days it seemed that anything would be better than the endless suspense.

One day near the end of August, Mark came bounding downstairs excitedly. "The radio just announced that women and children can leave. Saddam Hussein has guaranteed their safety. Do you think he means it?"

Del started upstairs to a phone. "I don't know, but I'm going to call the embassy to find out."

Other American women must have heard the announcement, too, because the embassy line was busy for a long time. When she finally got through, Del discovered that the ambassador had no evacuation plans and that he didn't even know if the announcement was true. They were again counseled to keep a low profile.

When Luisa called the British embassy, they promised to

be in touch as soon as they knew anything. At 6:00 p.m. Monday, they called her.

"We have arranged for an evacuation of British women and children tomorrow. We feel that Hussein's offer is genuine. Perhaps he figures that if he gets the women and children out of the way, there will be fewer repercussions from the West when he makes further moves. And of course, every person who leaves is one less mouth to feed.

"At any rate, Miss Lane, we're arranging for a convoy of women and children and a few Middle Easterners with British passports to travel overland to Baghdad and fly out. The convoy will meet at 6:00 a.m. tomorrow. Should we put your name on the list? We strongly advise that you leave. We're expecting all-out war over this invasion."

Luisa hesitated. "I don't know. Do you really think it's necessary to leave? I've got a job here, and all my things are here. If there's a chance this might blow over, I'd rather stay."

The British officer cleared his throat. "If you do, you will not be under the protection of Great Britain," he warned her. "You really should leave when you can."

"All right," Luisa conceded. "Put my name on the list."

"Good show," the officer said approvingly. "We'll see you tomorrow."

Luisa hung up and began telling Mark and Del what she had learned.

"Do you think Del and the boys could go with you?" Mark asked eagerly. "Please call them back and see if they'd let them go too. You could help Del with the boys, and you'd all get out."

Luisa dialed the British embassy again.

"As you know, I've been staying with the Endens, an American family," she said. "Their embassy has no evacuation plans. Could she and the children come with me? She has three little boys, and it would really help if I could assist her with the children when she leaves."

The British official answered quickly.

"That would be fine, Miss Lane. We have one other American woman already—Sherry, I think her name is. If Mrs. Enden wants to go, we'll add her and the three boys to our transportation list. Just let us know her decision by tonight."

Luisa hung up the phone and ran to find Del.

"The British embassy says you and the boys are welcome to go with me, and there's another American woman going. Do you want to go? Can you be ready by morning?"

Del stood staring at her friend. She could leave. The boys could leave. But what about Mark? The Iraqis would never let him go. Should she leave him? Or should the family stay together? She had no idea what to do.

Calling the American embassy again, Del asked their advice.

"Go for it," the American official replied. "Get out if you can. You have our blessing."

Now *she* had to decide. Mark urged her to take the kids and leave. "I may find a way to escape by myself," he pointed out, "but we could hardly disguise this whole family. I'd feel better if you and the boys were safely in America."

Suddenly Del's stomach began churning and cramping. She ran to the bathroom and shut the door, crying and praying and trying to get her rebellious digestive tract to settle down. If they had no children, she'd have known what to do. She'd stay with Mark. But did she have a right to jeopardize her children's lives by keeping them here?

Kneeling by the tub, she sobbed out her confusion to the Lord. "If You want me to go, God, You'll have to make it clear. And You know I always pack twice as much as I need. This time I can only take two suitcases apiece, and I'd better take less than that. It's vital that I pack the right things. Only You know what those things are. I don't. I can't even think."

As she prayed and wept, midnight arrived. Gradually an insistent chanting noise caught her attention. She wiped her eyes and emerged from the bathroom.

"What's going on?" She looked anxiously toward the covered window.

"I think it has something to do with organized passive resistance," Mark replied. "All the Kuwaitis are on their rooftops, chanting in unison. Listen!"

As she concentrated, Del clearly heard the chant grow louder. "Allah Akbar! Allah Akbar! Allah Akbar!"

"That means 'God is great,' " she mused. "They use that phrase a lot in prayer. Surely the Iraqis can't object to praising God."

Suddenly gunfire broke the chanting. Iraqi guards began shooting wildly at the rooftops. Screams filled the night, the screams of a child and a woman. Then sobbing, drowned by the rising chant. It sounded as if a child had been shot.

"This is crazy," she thought. "I've got to get my kids out of here."

Wiping at tears that wouldn't stop, Del walked into the bedroom and began pulling suitcases out of the closet. Mark came in and wrapped his arms around her.

"Guess you're going, huh?" he asked gently.

She burst into fresh sobs and buried her face in his shoulder.

"Yes, I guess. But I don't want to. I don't know what to do. I think the Lord wants us to go. But how can I leave you here? What if I never see you again?"

Mark held her, smoothing back her hair to kiss her forehead. He spoke lightly.

"Oh, you'll see me again. You won't get rid of me this easily! Maybe I can dress like a Kuwaiti and just walk out of town. Or disguise myself as an Indian. I learned to speak a little Urdu in Pakistan, you know. Listen, honey, the Lord has taken care of us this far. He'll get us together again. We'll just have to trust Him."

Del dried her eyes and resumed packing, thinking aloud.
"Tell Luisa to call the British embassy and put our
names on their list. Bring me the other big suitcase from
the kids' closet. There's no way I can manage three boys
and eight suitcases! I must cut down on luggage. I need to
handle whatever I take—and there's the backpack for carrying the baby and Portacrib too. I'm not going to take any
valuables because I don't think I could stand watching
someone confiscate them. I'd rather leave them here and
lose them than have them forcibly taken away."

The next few hours Del cried, packed, and prayed. The
chanting and shooting went on until 2:00 a.m., when the
demonstration ended. Soon she had one large suitcase full
of essentials for all four of them; another bag loaded with
extra clothing for the children; one small case of her own
personal items; a knapsack containing food, water, coloring
books, crayons, and toys; the backpack for carrying Loren;
and four small blankets. The last items were an after-
thought. Who knew where or how they'd be sleeping? If
they were on a bare floor, a blanket might come in handy.
Even though she'd packed only the barest essentials, when
assembled in one place, her luggage seemed like a small
mountain.

"How will I ever manage it?" she wondered. "I'm sure to
lose something vital."

Then for an hour she alternately paced, cried, and
hugged her husband. At four she woke the boys and began
dressing them, guiding their sleepy heads and arms into
their T-shirts. They ate a quick breakfast, made a final
bathroom stop, and began loading the Mitsubishi. Realizing
they were leaving Daddy and the safety of home, Eric and
Ryan began crying. Loren chimed in, just on general princi-
ples.

Del laughed through her tears. "Hush up, you two," she
scolded. "You've made Loren cry. Daddy will come to us as
soon as he can. And Jesus will be with us all. Remember

your Sabbath School song—'Angels Watching Over Me'?"

Mark looked at her with love in his eyes.

"That's my girl. Keep your chin up and trust in the Lord. I'll do the same, and we'll all be together again before long. I'm safe here in the apartment, and I've got enough food for six months. I'm going to build a little hiding place among those boxes of books on the third floor so I can hole up if I need to. I'm so glad Luisa's with you to help with the kids. Let me hear from you as soon as you can because I'll be worried until I know you're safely home."

After a final prayer, the women and children piled into the car. Luisa sat in front, her ginger tabby in a cage on her lap. Piled around her were kitty litter, cat food, two big suitcases, and somewhere there, Baby Loren. Del sat in back with the other boys and heaps of luggage, dabbing at her eyes and waving as the car pulled away from the house.

Proshad took them first to Luisa's apartment so that she could pick up a few more things and leave Bubble with an Iranian neighbor. Waiting for her in the car, Del felt ready to burst with tension. Why was Luisa taking so long? When Luisa returned, wiping away tears, Del could see that she had been having a real struggle to leave her pet, not knowing if she'd ever see him again.

With no cat to hold, Luisa took over the driving. Little Eric watched her intently in the rearview mirror for a moment and then said, "Was that the man who takes care of cats?"

Luisa nodded.

Eric leaned over the seat and patted her tenderly.

"Then Bubble will be OK, Luisa. Don't worry about him."

His loving concern comforted her.

"Can't you drive any faster?" asked Del frantically. "We'll miss the bus, and then what will we do?"

"Calm down, Del," Luisa soothed. "We've got plenty of time yet. It's only five fifteen, and we don't have to be there till six. Relax!"

Del tried, but her lack of sleep, intestinal upset, and fear made relaxing nearly impossible. She didn't really calm down until they arrived at their destination and saw dozens of passengers waiting for buses that had not yet arrived. That gave them time to start getting acquainted with their traveling companions, including the other American, Sherry.

"Why do you think Hussein decided to let us go?" one woman asked.

Luisa laughed. "I think it was because Margaret Thatcher said on TV that he was hiding behind women and children. Whatever caused it, I'm sure that all the prayers on our behalf had something to do with it too."

There was much anxiety over a teenaged British school-boy who was attempting to leave with the women and children. Everyone wondered if he'd be allowed to go. And if he got to Baghdad, would he be given an exit permit—or held as a human shield? Some of the Iraqi soldiers were barely in their teens, far younger than this British boy.

"And what was going on during the night?" a young mother inquired, setting her toddler on a suitcase while she rose to stretch.

"The Kuwaitis were on the rooftops chanting. Mark said it was a passive resistance thing," Del informed her.

"But what about the gunfire?" the woman persisted. "I heard people crying."

One of the British officials spoke up.

"Unfortunately, some Kuwaitis were shot during the demonstration. I don't know that it was intentional, but the soldiers were shooting at the rooftops to break up the demonstration, and people were killed."

"I'm glad we're leaving," said Del. "I just wish those buses would get here. They're almost an hour late. I wonder if we really will get out."

Chapter 7

The Long Way Home

In spite of Del's doubts, the buses did arrive, and the passengers boarded shortly after 7:00 a.m. Right away they discovered that the vehicles were not air conditioned. And although the group was making an all-day journey, the buses had no toilets. Mothers began to worry, especially when, instead of heading for Baghdad, the convoy began winding through the city, stopping here and there to pick up other passengers. It was 10:00 a.m. before they left town, and the heat was steadily increasing. Crying babies and fussy children added to the discomfort.

By noon they reached the Iraq/Kuwait border, and there in the sweltering heat, they sat for an hour and a half, waiting for permission to leave the country.

"I think the restrooms are over there," Del told Luisa quietly. "I'm going to take the boys. When I get back, I'll hold Loren, and you can go."

The young mother made her way to the front of the bus, lifting the boys over suitcases in the aisle and stepping around bundles that protruded from beneath the seats. In the restroom, she lingered at the sink, washing the boys' faces and her own in the tepid water. Outside, she bought bottled drinks for herself and the children and then reluctantly reboarded the bus to hold Loren so Luisa could leave. It had felt so good to get up and walk around! Her self-pity evaporated, however, when she saw a very pregnant young woman awkwardly maneuvering her way off and on the bus.

Just as the buses were about to roll, Iraqi officials halted the convoy, boarded each bus, and asked the same question. "We are looking for an American schoolboy. He is wanted for questioning. Would the American schoolboy please come forward?"

Passengers on Del's bus shook their heads and shrugged their shoulders. They knew nothing about any such person. The British schoolboy slid lower in his seat and kept very still. At last the officials called off their search and signaled the drivers to proceed. Everyone heaved a sigh of relief. The boy wasn't out of Iraq yet, but at least he was out of Kuwait!

With the convoy underway again, the hot desert wind, which at first had felt good blowing in the open windows, began to suck the moisture from their bodies and deposit fine sand over everything. Del envied the wealthy British woman whose chauffeured car followed at the end of the caravan. In air-conditioned comfort, she was leaving Kuwait in style!

Before long the children were begging for water. Del gave them some from her limited supply and tried to get them to sleep. At lunchtime, they discovered that the cheese slices in the knapsack had melted, so they had pita-bread cheese-melts.

"Very fancy," Del pointed out, making the best of the situation.

"That's not the only thing melting," Luisa added, pointing to a yellow box. "The crayons in that bag are melting too."

As the bus bounced over the rough road, some children began throwing up. There was no possibility of stopping.

The mothers did their best, but soon, the entire bus was smelling of sickness and dirty diapers. Those who weren't ill already felt queasy because of the odors.

At six that evening the buses made another restroom stop. Del discovered that she had been sweating so profusely that her body had no water to eliminate. Realizing the danger of dehydration, she pushed the children to drink more than they wanted. Back on the road again, they ate the rest of the bread and melted cheese and called it supper.

The convoy didn't stop again until it reached Baghdad at midnight. By then the temperature had begun to cool. At the Al Rashid Hotel, the passengers with their luggage formed an orderly line in front of the main desk. When they reached it, they were given a room without having to sign or pay for anything. Presumably the embassy was caring for the cost.

Leaving Luisa to get their rooms, Del scribbled a quick note to Mark and ran out to find the British woman's private car.

"Please call this number when you get back to Kuwait," she begged the chauffeur, "and let my husband know I got here OK. Here's a note for him. Deliver it if you can, but if you can't, please call at least. He was so worried."

The chauffeur looked at her kindly. "I'll tell him," he promised, tucking the note into his pocket.

Back inside, Del and Luisa dragged the children and luggage to their separate rooms. When she saw that the bathroom had a deep tub, Del filled it and popped all three boys in to soak, thinking as much of getting moisture back into their skins as of getting the dirt off!

After they were clean, she had prayers with them and tucked them into bed about 3:00 a.m. Though exhausted, Del felt too keyed up to relax. She knew that in the morning she would need to get exit papers for herself and the children. She didn't sleep.

In the morning, she noticed that the British seemed rather anxious about having Americans in their group. Not wanting to endanger them in any way, she decided to split from the British, leave Luisa with the boys for the morning, and go with the other American woman to try to get exit permits. This wasn't something she was accustomed to doing. Mark usually got the permits and papers while she watched the boys. Now she had to find her way around this hostile city.

Breathing a prayer for guidance, she asked the hotel to call a taxi, and she and Sherry headed to Iraqi Immigration. To their relief, the driver took them to the right place, and before long, they had exit permits. In filling out the forms, however, Del had to list her Kuwaiti address. She did so, praying that no one would check there for her missing husband.

The taxi was still waiting for them when they emerged from the office, so they instructed the driver to take them to the American embassy to check on available flights for American citizens. When they arrived, they discovered that they had just missed a French flight and would have to wait for another plane.

"We're sorry," said the secretary. "Why don't you two women go back to the hotel and get your bags packed; we'll have our driver pick you up and take you to the ambassador's house. She's left the country, but her staff can care for you there."

When the taxi let them off at the hotel, Luisa welcomed Del with relief. "I'm so glad you're back," she said. "Here are your boys, safe and sound. Wish I could say the same for myself! They are hyper today. I had visions of your being taken captive and leaving me with these three wild monkeys forever!

"I need to get my own paperwork cared for now, so I'm afraid you'll be on your own. I tried to call my family in England, and I actually got through—but when I started speaking in English, the connection was cut. Not to worry, though. I'll be home soon, I hope."

Before Luisa left, she and Del hugged and prayed together, promising to contact one another as soon as they were safely at their homes.

When the embassy car arrived, the two American women and three boys, plus all their luggage, squeezed into it. At their destination, Del was struck by the contrast of going from an uncomfortable desert bus to a beautiful ambassadorial residence—all within twenty-four hours.

"Sensory overload," Del thought. "I'm too tired to enjoy all this." Still, she and the boys got some sleep that night.

In the morning, when she felt better, Del decided to enjoy the swimming pool. Seeing how weary the mother was, some of the men on the ambassador's staff took pity on her and played with the boys. When she fell asleep in her deck chair, they kept the children entertained with coloring books and crayons.

The next morning she packed immediately. Del and Sherry had been told they should be ready to leave at any time. The morning dragged on with no word of a departure time from the airport.

"Have you heard anything about the British group?" Del asked an attaché. "Did they all get out? What about that schoolboy?"

The attaché shook his head.

"They all got exit permits," he said, "and your friend Luisa and the boy got them, too, but the Iraqis could still stop him at the airport. They've done that before."

"Oh, I pray they'll be safe," Del exclaimed. "I hope we'll all be out of here by this time tomorrow."

"I met some people at the hotel who've been here a week waiting for a plane," said Sherry dryly. "You've got a lot of faith!"

"I have a lot to base it on," Del replied. "You wouldn't believe all the things the Lord has done for us the past month! We're going to get out of here, I just *know* it!"

At noon the staff served lunch, and Del had resigned herself to another day in Iraq, when an attaché dashed in.

"Get your suitcases. There's a plane leaving at two o'clock, and they said there's room for you."

Quickly Del loaded her bags and the boys into the embassy car, where Sherry and a driver waited. At the airport, they boarded an Iraqi Air jet for the flight to Turkey. As the plane climbed into the sky, the passengers were quiet. Still in Iraqi hands, they did not yet feel free.

In Ankara, Turkey, the plane stopped on the tarmac away from the terminal. Passengers disembarked and walked to the nearby Canadian Airlines 747 that awaited them. A representative from the American embassy met Del.

"Mrs. Enden?" he asked, eyeing the three little boys. "I've been told to check on you and to help you in any way that I can. Are there any people in the United States that you want me to contact about your arrival time?"

Del was touched by his thoughtfulness and pleased that the American government, as well as the Lord, was looking out for her.

This time, as the plane lifted into the air, a cheer rose from the passengers. At last they felt free! When the aircraft reached its cruising altitude, the flight attendants began bustling up and down the aisles, laughing, smiling, and offering congratulations, champagne, and soft drinks. To Del it felt more like a party than a trip!

When she discovered there was room enough on the plane so each child could have a whole row of seats, Del thanked the Lord. But because all three never seemed to be asleep at the same time, she got little rest herself. Shortly after the boys finally fell asleep, the plane landed in London, and everyone was asked to disembark.

"Please, can't I stay here?" Del begged. "The boys just got to sleep."

The flight attendant looked at the young mother's weary face and nodded her permission. Even then, Del got no sleep, for another U.S. government employee boarded the plane to question her at length about the invasion and the family's conditions while in hiding. After he left, passengers began reboarding, and the plane headed for Toronto.

Near midnight, they arrived at the Toronto airport. Again, an embassy representative sought her out, cleared her through customs, and took her to a beautiful hotel. She was so thankful for help with luggage and transportation.

"Just relax and get some sleep," the official urged. "Here's some cash in case you need it. We'll try to get you a flight to the States tomorrow. Welcome to freedom!"

Del felt well cared for but exhausted. She had hardly closed her eyes for almost three days. Having slept all night, however, the boys weren't about to sleep again. Del simply tried to keep them quiet until the other guests rose. Since they were all ravenous, she called room service and ordered just about everything vegetarian on the menu. The boys and their mother sat down to a feast of Cheerios, French fries, scrambled eggs, and pancakes. By the time they had eaten all they could hold, it was nearly nine o'clock.

Del dialed the embassy. "How fast can you get me on a plane to Philadelphia?" she begged. "I know you planned to send me later, but the boys won't sleep, and I've had little rest in three days. If I could just get home to my mother, I could crash."

The secretary hesitated. Something in this woman's voice sounded desperate. "I'll see what I can do and call you back," she replied. An hour later the embassy called. "There's space available on a noon flight," the secretary told her. "Can you be ready that fast?"

"I'm ready right *now*!" Del answered. "Come and get us!"

During the next half-hour, Del packed again and put through a long-distance call to her mother. "Mom? It's me, Del."

"Del!" her mother fairly shouted. "Are you in Canada? We've been getting messages every couple of hours from the State Department. Del and the boys left Baghdad! Del and the boys left Ankara! Del and the boys left London! I've been sending back messages everywhere asking if you needed money. Do you? What's going on?"

"Yes, we're in Toronto, Mom, and we don't need money. The embassy is taking care of our expenses. I didn't call earlier because I didn't want to wake you up when I didn't know what our plans were. We're leaving on a noon flight to Philadelphia. Can you meet us there about four-thirty?"

Her mother's joy came over the lines so clearly that Del wanted to cry. But not now. She had to hang on a little longer.

"Of *course* I'll be there! I can't wait to get my arms around you and those boys."

Del laughed wearily. "I can't wait to give them to you, Mom. I'm so tired. Don't plan a thing for me. I just want to sleep."

Dragging her bags and the boys, Del stumbled through the Toronto airport and onto the jet.

"Just another four hours," she told herself. Then later, "Just another two hours." The boys, at times, were impossible, but she didn't have the strength to scold them.

When they landed, she waited until the plane was almost empty before struggling out of the aircraft and into the lounge area. She looked anxiously around. Not one familiar face did she see. The boys were whining, Loren was crying, and Del felt like sitting right down and bawling with him.

Then she saw her mother, running up the corridor. "I couldn't find a parking place," she panted. "But I'm here now, honey, I'm here."

Del fell into her mother's arms, tears running down her cheeks. How they got through customs and into the car, she couldn't remember, but by suppertime, they were at the Joneses' farm near Reading. Del's parents took care of their lively grandchildren while Del took a long, hot shower and crawled into bed. For the first twenty-four hours, she did little else but sleep.

How thankful she was for loving Christian parents who had prayed her through this ordeal! For freedom! And for God's protection on the grueling trip home. If Mark were only here, everything would be perfect.

Back in Kuwait, the friendly chauffeur phoned Mark to let him know that his wife had arrived unharmed in Baghdad. It was another three weeks, however, before Mark learned that she and the boys were safely in America.

Chapter 8
Resistance Action

With the women and children evacuated, Iraqi forces began tightening their hold on Kuwait City. The United States had been ordered to close its embassy because—according to Iraq—Kuwait was no longer a separate country in need of an embassy. The embassy in Baghdad could handle anything that needed to be cared for in this nineteenth province of Iraq! When the ambassador refused to close down the facility, troops surrounded the compound in an attempt to starve them out.

Mark still had no idea whether Del had made it safely home. One day he heard that an African friend who worked at a local hotel was going to Baghdad to apply for an exit permit. Quickly he called him.

"Ibrahim, if they still have international phone lines in Baghdad, would you call my wife's parents in America to see if she arrived safely? I'll give you her phone number and the money for the call."

Ibrahim agreed. He was anxious to get out himself. He'd watched Iraqi officials bring into the hotel Westerners who were headed for Baghdad to be human shields. Indeed, he had helped one of them escape and had promised Mark that if he were ever caught and brought to his hotel, he'd try to assist him too.

His African passport made it possible for him to cross the Kuwait border and travel to Baghdad easily. There he obtained his exit permit and called Del. It took her a few seconds to understand who he was and to understand that Mark was still safe and well. She assured Ibrahim that she and the boys were fine and thanked him profusely.

The next day, back in Kuwait, Ibrahim called Mark. "I talked to your wife. She says she is fine, and she loves you," he reported. "She said to tell you that your church is trying to get you released."

"I can't thank you enough, my friend," Mark told him. "It's been three weeks since she left, and I've been almost crazy with worry."

That night Mark thanked the Lord for answered prayer and again claimed God's promises of protection for himself.

After Del left, Mark's spirits plummeted. He knew that in filling out her exit papers in Baghdad, his wife would have had to list her previous address. Knowing that the Iraqis might have that information now, he spent much of the next week hiding in closets just in case they followed up the lead. This did nothing to raise his morale!

Without Del and the children, the house seemed empty and bleak. Mark hauled out the nineteen boxes of books that had been so recently cleared as part of his household shipment and began reading the books methodically. Like his wife, however, he found it hard to concentrate in the midst of such threatening uncertainty. Still, he tried to read. Biographies of Lincoln, Jefferson, and John Quincy Adams distracted him for a while, but he found Sherlock Holmes easier reading!

One day he picked up *The Diary of Anne Frank*, but he soon put it down. It was too real. Mark remembered that the book ended with the Nazis finding her family's hideout and capturing them. He didn't even want to think about that, so he buried the book in the bottom of the box and didn't touch it again.

Other books were more helpful. *The Desire of Ages* and *Steps to Christ* he read again and again, savoring the sense of peace they brought. He studied his Bible and read the Koran, comparing the two and learning all he could about the Muslims' holy book.

Mark began spending more time contacting other Americans as part of the underground Resistance. Calls were spaced far apart and kept brief to prevent anyone from tracing a call to its source. Kuwaiti Resistance kept track of the foreigners in hiding and worked to provide safe places and essentials for them.

Two houses away, three Britishers were discovered and taken to Baghdad. It seemed that whenever the TV broadcast that government leaders such as Edward Heath or Yasuhiro Nakasone of Japan had come to Baghdad on peace missions and persuaded Saddam Hussein to release into their custody a group of hostages, part of Kuwait City would be sealed off the next day and the same number of Westerners rounded up to replace the ones who left! Those in hiding began dreading the visits of well-meaning diplomats!

Other than that, the taking of hostages seemed to follow no systematic pattern. It appeared, rather, to be random searches and accidental discoveries. Some Westerners gave themselves up because they were running out of supplies or patience. For them, anxiety over the unknown outweighed the dangers of surrender. Feeling that they could not face waking up another morning to wonder whether they'd be caught that day, those Westerners walked out into the street and gave themselves up.

Although the American embassy was under siege, the phones still worked most of the time. This enabled the staff to keep in touch with Americans in hiding, and they, in turn, could receive and send overseas messages via the embassy.

Diesel generators within the compound ran for one hour a day, enough to charge batteries and run communication lines. Once a week Mark could call in a two-line message for Del. Once a week he might receive a similar message back. Del's messages sometimes hinted at progress being made toward Mark's release, but she couldn't say anything about specific plans. And often, the messages just didn't get through. Del never knew whether it was a communication problem or whether Mark was in trouble. She agreed with her husband's opinion included in one letter: "They say that no news is good news. I choose to pick an argument with whoever coined that ridiculous phrase!"

Although he talked to others on the phone, Mark felt isolated and alone. As if the Lord knew he needed a boost, the young man received a call from the Resistance. It seemed that they were trying to relocate an American man whose hiding place was threatened. Could Mark accommodate him? Mark readily agreed.

Ron arrived in Kuwait the day before the invasion on a two-day business trip for the Chiquita Banana Company. He was now hiding in an apartment situated along the Gulf Road, an area that was being systematically taken over building after building by the invading army. Realizing he was about to be caught, Ron called the embassy, which put him in touch with the Resistance for help. They agreed to assist him in moving to Mark's apartment.

Two cars came with Ron, the first filled with Kuwaitis to show him the way and to act as a decoy in case of problems at checkpoints. Ron drove the second. On the highway the cars became separated by truckloads of Iraqi soldiers. Ron sat frozen in the front seat, looking doggedly at the road while the idle troops in the back of the truck ahead scrutinized him.

"Any minute now," he thought, trying to control his pulse and breathing. "Will they take me prisoner or shoot me?"

When the cars finally turned off the highway onto Mark's

street, Ron found himself hyperventilating!

As Mark helped to haul the American's belongings upstairs, he was delighted to find that Ron had brought with him boxes of fresh fruit intended for use as samples to encourage Kuwaiti grocery stores to carry Chiquita fruit. Apples, pears, and bananas filled the refrigerator. Just their smell alone had Mark drooling. In addition to the fruit, Ron added to the pantry fifty cans of beans, dried milk, and a six-week supply of juices.

Mark was more than glad to have a roommate to distract his mind and keep him company. The men were good for one another, balancing each other's mood swings and helping to stave off depression. They quickly developed a routine of listening to news, reading, eating, playing music, and watching TV. To keep up their strength, they exercised faithfully every day—fifty pushups, fifty jumping jacks, fifty sit-ups, and so on. Deliberately, they tried to live as normally as possible. During their private times, while Mark studied his Bible and Arabic lessons, Ron tried to master Spanish.

Mealtimes became a prolonged ritual made more enjoyable by the variety of fresh food Ron had brought. Oatmeal, of course, was a daily staple, and Mark fixed rice and lentils in more ways than Ron ever thought possible! One day, when Mark went on a clean-out-the-cupboards spree, he let out a shout.

"Ron! Guess what I found!"

"A nice, juicy steak?" Ron suggested slyly.

Mark made a face. "No, better than that! A box of peanut M&M's! And some Skittles! Let's party!"

The men divided the candy carefully, savoring each piece and marveling that such an insignificant event could lift their spirits.

Sometimes, when they were both feeling restless, Mark would suggest going on a hunt. Armed with bug spray, they would hunt through the house from top to bottom for carpenter ants and attack them vigorously, laughing at themselves over their war strategies against the insects.

On days when the humidity was high, the TV began receiving Bahrain's CNN newscasts. They began every afternoon and continued on the hour until 11:00 p.m., with a special two-hour recap after that. Since the broadcasts were in both Arabic and English, listening to them helped Mark's language study.

The men found they had many similar interests, cartoon shows being one of them. Laughing at Tom and Jerry or Looney Tunes seemed to ease the tension and helped them to see the funny side of their own predicament. Mark also had plenty of time to explore the intricacies of the Nintendo games he had bought the week before his Gulf trip, but he couldn't get Ron interested in playing computer games with him.

Best of all were the long discussions the men enjoyed, arguing and agreeing on a wide variety of topics from politics to Bible prophecy. When he discovered that Ron was a Methodist and had been studying the history of his denomination, Mark pointed out that Seventh-day Adventists had a Methodist heritage and showed him the similarities between the denominations.

The Westerners' telephone network continued to grow. Callers would listen carefully for any sign of depression in their contacts. If they detected any, the person received a shower of encouraging phone calls that day. In various parts of town, those in hiding established lookout points from their windows and roofs and relayed to one another information on movements and activities down the street or around the corner. With such an effective information system, most of the Westerners knew what was going on as soon as Iraqi intelligence did—and sometimes sooner!

At 5:30 one morning, Mark was awakened by shouts in the street. Peering out the window, he saw that the area had been cordoned off by Iraqi military.

"Ron!" he called. "Something's going on. Come and look!"

Ron joined him, peeking around the edge of the blackout paper. As they watched, soldiers stopped at every house up and down the street, knocking on doors and rounding up about thirty foreign men. They loaded them into trucks and headed in the direction of Baghdad. During the roundup, Mark expected a knock on his door at any moment, but somehow in the confusion, the church house was skipped.

"Thank You, Lord," Mark prayed. "I saw You at work today. Give me faith to continue believing You are still in control."

As time went on, the men found themselves listening to the news less and less. Perhaps it was because the broadcasts swung their emotions from hope to despair, depending on the day's events. But every night, from eleven to one in the morning, they listened to the two-hour CNN international news from Bahrain. It seemed to be the most accurate and complete newscast their television would pick up.

The Voice of America began broadcasting recorded messages from friends and relatives of those in hiding. Mark listened to them regularly, hoping to hear from Del, longing for the encouraging sound of her voice. With a New Zealander, he smuggled out a letter to Del, expressing his frustration on that score.

"One thing that's becoming a mystery to me is why I haven't heard a message from anyone on VOA. Please read my lips when I write this down—I would love to hear *something*. I've tried to make it a ritual each day to listen to the program called 'Messages From Home.' So far, that habit has left me unrewarded, and it's a habit I guess I will have to soon desert. Is anyone there? Please? Please try to send a message at least once a week. If you can't do this, then at least assign the task to someone who can. (I just read the above paragraph and realize how awful it sounds. Please don't take it wrong. I just feel so alone, and there are only a few things to hang on to that help the time pass with hope.)"

His vigil was finally rewarded when he heard Del's voice over the radio. He became so excited and noisy that Ron had to hush him. Weekly he sent his two-line messages through the embassy, and fourteen times he sent out letters to Del with various groups of foreigners who were allowed to leave at different stages of the occupation. Some letters got to her, but most didn't. Once, however, the Resistance brought him a fax message from Del. The next day, they delivered a letter to Ron from his wife Kate. Those two brief communications brightened the week for both of them and infused them with new courage to continue their hiding.

To keep up morale, some members of the phone network began publishing a little news sheet full of humorous material. Kuwaiti Resistance delivered it to those in hiding, along with fresh food and money. The jokes and cartoons it contained triggered much-needed laughter.

For over three weeks, Mark shared by phone the excitement and fear of an American named Tom. Tom had been working for the Kuwaiti military and was particularly wanted by the Iraqis for his expertise in programming and firing Hawk missiles for defense against enemy aircraft. On the first day of the invasion, the Kuwait army had successfully shot down about forty-five Iraqi aircraft, using the Hawk missiles. When the invaders captured the military supplies, they trucked more than two hundred Hawks back to Baghdad for their own use. But they really needed Tom to show them how the missiles operated.

When the soldiers broke into his apartment, Tom slid under the bed. Not finding him, they posted a guard at the entrance to wait for him to return. All day Tom lay quietly under the bed. That night, when the guard left, Tom came out and began preparing a place for himself to hide in the large air-conditioning ducts above his apartment. He rigged up a rope ladder on which he could climb into the duct work. Carefully he hauled into the large pipes packages of dried pasta, bottles of liquor, a radio, pillows, blankets, and finally, his little terrier puppy. Then he pulled the ladder up after him and replaced the ceiling tile.

Soldiers searched the building from top to bottom without finding him. Some of them moved into the empty apartments, including Tom's. He amused himself by watching them through the ceiling cracks. It annoyed him to see them using his things and trashing his apartment, but he kept still, knowing that his life was at stake.

He kept the puppy calm and sleepy with frequent swigs of liquor, using the same tactic on himself. Munching on the dried pasta staved off hunger for both of them. Together they snuggled beneath the blankets, keeping one another warm, for the cold air coming through the ducts threatened them with hypothermia. Tom thought how ironic it was that he might die of cold when it was 130 degrees outside!

During the day, when the building was empty, Tom would swing out of the attic, use the bathroom, help himself to whatever food was available, and phone Mark to let him know he was still alive. Then he'd climb back into the duct work, retrieve his ladder, and spend another twenty-four hours in hiding.

Once he called to report he'd nearly been caught. He was in the bathroom when the soldiers came back unexpectedly. He jumped behind the bathroom door when they opened it, and fortunately for him, they didn't close the door when they got inside but used the toilet and left. Tom went back into hiding as fast as possible.

On another occasion, he didn't have time to pull up the rope ladder and had to leave it hanging down in the corner of the room. Although someone came into the room, he didn't notice the ladder, and Tom escaped detection again.

Nearly every day, he could get to a phone sometime and call Mark. Some days he could talk five or ten minutes, others only a few seconds. For fun and security, Mark answered his phone differently each time. Tom never knew if he'd hear a simulated Indian voice answering in Urdu, a heavy Filipino accent, stilted Middle Eastern English such as, "Hallo! I am very happy to hear from you. How is your health? What is the time by your watch?" or, "Allo! Iraqi High Command! Saddam Hussein's Headquarters!" Whatever the response, the phone calls always gave Tom a lift.

One night he watched through the ceiling cracks as some uniformed men dismantled his electronic equipment and carted it away. The next morning, when they had gone, he scouted through the building, found his equipment in the servants' quarters, and retrieved it. Before he could get it back into the duct work, however, he had to scurry back into hiding.

Puzzled at finding the equipment back in the apartment, the men carted it off again. The next day he found it and almost had it up in the ceiling, when they returned and he had to flee. Finally, on the third try, he managed to pull everything up into his hiding place. Watching the reactions of the soldiers below as they puzzled over the disappearance of the equipment, he found it hard to keep from laughing aloud!

After Tom didn't report in for five days, the other Westerners feared for his life. When he did call, it was to say that the Iraqis had taken everything that could be moved from the apartment building. Sinks, electric wires from the walls, light fixtures, carpeting, furniture, and finally, the toilets. At this juncture, Tom decided it was time to move.

"I've been hiding here for twenty-three days now," he told Mark. "My food is used up, and now they've ripped the pipes out so I can't get any more water. But taking the john is just the last straw. I can't hide here any longer. Would you contact the Resistance and see if they can move me somewhere else?"

The next day Kuwaiti Resistance quietly transferred Tom and his puppy to a safer location.

Another incident set the American community rocking with laughter. Two American men and one Britisher were housed in the same apartment building. During a roundup, soldiers ordered the three of them to pack suitcases and prepare to leave. They went back to their apartments, the two Americans going into one, and the Britisher into the other. Once inside, the six-foot-four American rebelled.

"I'm just not going to let them take me like that," he sputtered. "At least I can try to escape." And with that, he slid under the bed and lay quietly.

The other man looked around and to his alarm saw his friend's feet sticking out well beyond the bottom of the bed. At the same time he heard the clomp of military boots coming down the hall.

Thinking quickly, he began to sing. "Your feet are show-ing under the bed, my friend. Pull them in, or your life will end. Your feet are out in the air, my friend . . ."

Just in the nick of time, the feet disappeared. The guard walked through the doorway, watching the crazy American who was packing and singing merrily. He picked up his suitcase, smiled at the guard, and said, "OK. Let's go." As they left the room, he carefully closed the door.

Later on, Bigfoot, as he was nicknamed, joined other Americans in hiding in Kuwait and told the story, laughing appreciatively at his friend's quick wit. The other two men turned up in Baghdad at the end of the war, having been held hostage for several months.

Various other national groups were getting their citizens out, and one day Proshad announced that he and his Indian friends and family would be leaving in a few weeks.

"We're all pooling our money," he told Mark. "We're sell-ing our cars and all our household goods. Some of the fam-ily has been earning good money cleaning up bombed buildings. I'm selling my things too. Things aren't much good if our lives are in danger. The Indian embassy has arranged a caravan to Jordan, and we can fly from there. But we have to have money for airfares."

Mark was sorry to see Rani and Proshad leave, for they

had been such a help to him. Proshad had brought in fresh food regularly and been their go-between with the water carrier, thus keeping their presence concealed. It would be hard without them. Still, he wished them well.

"Here," he said to Proshad. "I'll contribute some of my electronic equipment. Sell this VCR along with your things. I just wish I could get out with you!"

When the day came for the Indians to leave, Mark gave Proshad some money and a telephone number in Pennsylvania where he could reach Del.

"When you're out, please call Del and tell her you and Rani are safe and that I am fine, will you?"

Proshad nodded solemnly. "I certainly will. I won't forget. I have enjoyed working for you and so has Rani. Come to India sometime and see us! We'll make you some good curry!"

"I'll bet you would," Mark laughed, hugging Proshad. "God bless you and keep you all safe."

That night it was even harder to concentrate on reading. Del and the boys were gone. Luisa was gone. Rani and Proshad were gone—why couldn't *he* go? He felt so left out—like the one kid who didn't get a Christmas present! Still, he was thankful for Ron's company.

Six weeks after Ron moved in, a radio broadcast announced the release of all Frenchmen. Ron came to life.

"Maybe I can get out with that group!" he exclaimed. "I speak fluent French. I'm going to call the French embassy and see if they'll claim me."

Dialing the French embassy, he spoke fluently, persuading them to give him a passport and let him go out with their group. The morning he left, he gave Mark $500 in cash, some equipment, and the rest of the food. Then he threw his arms around him.

"You've saved my life, buddy," he declared. "As soon as I get out, I'll get to work on getting you released. The Chiquita Company has a regular team set up to handle such crises. We work in so many different countries, there's always someone in trouble. And I'll get your letter to Del if I get out myself. Wish me luck!"

"Not just luck," Mark said with a smile. "God bless!"

Speaking only French, Ron made his way to the Kuwaiti military air base and boarded the Iraqi plane that was to fly the Frenchmen to Baghdad on the first leg of their journey to freedom. At Baghdad, where they changed planes, an immigration officer inspected his papers before giving him an exit permit. To Ron's horror, the officer spotted an error in his forged papers. His place of birth was still listed as "Omaha."

"Where is 'Omaha'?" the frowning officer asked in French.

Ron swallowed hard and put on his most convincing French accent.

"It's a place in France. Remember Omaha Beach in World War II?"

The officer nodded and stamped the passport.

As he boarded the plane to leave, Ron found himself hyperventilating again!

Chapter 9
Plots and Plans

After Ron left, Mark became extremely depressed, refusing to answer the phone all day. The next day, when he picked it up, his network contact scolded him soundly for worrying everyone.

"What's wrong with you?" he demanded. "We thought you'd been captured."

"I didn't want to talk to anybody," Mark confessed. "I just felt rotten. It seems like everybody's getting out but me. I haven't heard from Del for ages. Besides, I've got a toothache that just won't quit."

The contact softened his tone.

"We're all going to get out of here if we keep our heads," he declared confidently. "I'll see if we can find you a dentist. Hang in there, fellow. And don't turn yourself in. As long as you're in hiding, you've got a chance."

Mark hung up. How did that guy know he'd been thinking of surrendering? He had toyed with the idea of just walking out into the street and stopping the tanks as they passed. Anything seemed preferable to the endless waiting.

Still, if he was going to stay in hiding, it might be a good idea to have an alternate plan. He decided to prepare himself a more secure spot.

On the third floor was a large room filled with two hundred boxes of books. Carefully, Mark rearranged them, forming a winding tunnel through the books to the far corner of the room. In a large space surrounded on all sides by boxes, he placed a sleeping bag, a week's supply of nonperishable food, water, books, money, and a shortwave radio. If the apartment was searched, he planned to run upstairs, dive into the tunnel, pull a couple of boxes in behind himself to block the entrance, and hole up in the corner. Just having a plan made him feel more in control again.

In the days that followed, he spent three or four nights in the "cave" behind the books. There, reading his Bible by flashlight, he found a chapter that was to become his favorite—Psalm 143. Snatches of it penetrated his confused mind. "In thy faithfulness answer me." "The enemy has pursued me; he has crushed my life to the ground. . . . My spirit faints within me" (RSV). Mark wondered why God had let him have Del and the boys if he was going to lose his life in Kuwait! "Make haste to answer me, O Lord! my spirit fails!"

"You can say that again," he told the Lord. "My spirit fails, and my tooth aches! Can't You help me? I appreciated your sending Ron, but it seems like it's worse now that he's gone."

Mark read on to Psalm 145. It was more comforting. "The Lord . . . raises up all who are bowed down." "He will fulfill [their] desire . . . ; He will . . . hear their cry and will save them" (NASB).

"Lord," he prayed, "I'm certainly bowed down. You're the only one who can save me. Please do it quickly before I go crazy."

Every day Mark poured over his Bible, reading it through again and again. Just talking to the Lord and reading His promises brought some peace to his mind.

The Lord did answer his prayer about the aching tooth.

The Resistance sent a Danish dentist to visit him.

"You've got a badly infected tooth," the doctor declared after examining him. "What have you been doing for it?"

Mark shrugged. "At first I took aspirin, but it didn't touch it. Then the Resistance brought me some whiskey and told me to hold it in my mouth, and it would numb the pain. It did help, but mostly I just let the tooth hurt. It's been killing me!"

The dentist looked thoughtful.

"Well," he said, "I can bring a portable drill and work on the tooth if necessary, but let's try an antibiotic first. If that doesn't work, I'll bring the drill. You'll probably have to have a root canal done when you get back to the States, though."

The idea of a portable drill struck Mark with terror. Praying that the antibiotic would work, he gratefully accepted the prescription, and a Resistance agent filled it. To his relief, the antibiotic took care of the problem temporarily. The dentist was right, however. He had to have a root canal done six months later.

Now that Del was gone, Mark decided to pack up everything he wasn't using and lock it in Loren's room. He wrote about it in a letter to Eric.

I've been having fun going through cupboards and drawers. Most of our things that we are going to keep, I have packed away in our barrels and boxes. In going through your clothes, I found your pj's with the skeleton on them. Ooooo! It was spooky, but I enjoyed it. Did you get all dressed up at Halloween and go trick or treating?

When he found Ryan's superball, he sat down and wrote his oldest son a letter too.

Yesterday I found your little hard superball, the

one that bounces so high. Now I have a box full of your soccer balls, baseballs, football, and other things. I even have practiced a few kicks with the soccer ball to stay in shape so that when we get together we can play a game or two. You sure are good with your kicks, and you are very fast too. I will have to work extra hard to keep up with you. I have packed away our baseball mitts and the baseball, hoping that we can play with them as well. That would be fun.

As he wrote, it struck Mark that if these letters ever got through, they might be the last communication his sons would ever receive from him. The thought nearly overwhelmed him. He decided he'd better write to Loren too, although the toddler was barely two. Someday he might want to read his father's letter. So he wrote Loren, quoting for him the words of a Bill Gaither song, telling him how special he was and that God had made Loren "the only one of your kind."

After Ron left, Mark invited the remaining church members to come to church on Sabbath but to keep the assembly down to fifteen or less. They had been meeting in small home groups since the invasion, but as his was now the only life endangered by the meetings, he felt free to resume some sort of church service. He discovered that most of his members had fled the country. Those who came were depressed and fearful because of the atrocities being committed around them.

"Did you hear about that Pakistani family who tried to drive out the day after the invasion?" one man asked. "The man packed his car with food and water and took his wife, three boys, and a teenage daughter, and headed for the border. Thousands of other foreigners had the same idea, and the Pakistani family found themselves part of an eighty-mile line of cars waiting to clear immigration. They waited for days on the desert road, not daring to leave the line for fear of losing their place.

"Iraqi troops were still coming across the border on that same road, and one group took the family's food and water. Returning to Kuwait seemed too dangerous. There was always the hope that the line would speed up, and they'd soon be free. Day after day they sat baking in their car under the desert sun. The two older boys died of dehydration. The distraught parents dug graves for their boys and buried them beside the road. Then the men in one of the passing troop trucks spotted the teenage girl. Stopping the convoy, they snatched the girl from her family and drove off. No one's seen her since. The father managed to turn his car around on that narrow road and came back to Kuwait with his wife and little boy. He's nearly crazy with grief, blaming himself for everything and praying that his daughter will die quickly. What is *wrong* with people, Pastor?"

Mark looked away. He, too, had been asking why. That very week he had talked to a Kuwaiti man who worked at the local hospital.

"Did the invaders really take the babies out of the incubators like the news reported?" he asked the man. "Or is that just propaganda?"

The man shook his head sadly.

"No, Mr. Enden, it wasn't propaganda. I myself buried some of the babies. The incubators were loaded onto trucks headed for Baghdad. You remember that little boy you used to visit there?"

"Yes. His name was Obi, I think. A seven-year-old in a coma after a wreck. He was on life support. Don't tell me they took the machine!"

The man nodded.

That week he went back to his books and the Bible, seeking answers and comfort for the few members he had left. The next Sabbath he spoke about the origin of evil and why bad things happen to good people. The texts he read comforted him as well as his congregation.

The Lord had even more comfort in store for them that day. An Indian family from Goa who had been baptized just before Mark's arrival in the country arrived at church with a thrilling account of their activities. They said that after the invasion, they had invited neighbors into their home for daily Bible study and prayer. Running out of materials, they had stopped by the church two months before to borrow a Dukane projector and filmstrips. Now, they reported, they had a total of fifteen friends who had made decisions for Christ. The small band of believers rejoiced and held an impromptu thanksgiving service for the Lord's leading and this encouraging news.

Not long after that, Mark received a call from Jerry, an American who had been in strict hiding and hadn't talked to another person for five weeks. Now, however, he was desperate.

"The Iraqis have begun breaking into the apartments downstairs," he said frantically. "They seem to be gone right now, but if they come upstairs, they'll find me. You have ties with the Resistance. Can you get me out of here?"

"I'll do my best," Mark promised.

That night the Resistance moved Jerry in with Tom, the fellow who'd been hiding in the duct work. For the rest of the occupation, Americans chuckled about the pair and called frequently to check on "Tom and Jerry."

Others were not so fortunate. Don, a friend of Mark's, had made contact with some Iraqi soldiers. For a fee, they had given him compasses, desert gear, maps, and tide information. Mark and four other men began making plans to escape. Christmas was their deadline. In preparation for the move, the men hoped to move in with Don before Thanksgiving.

A Kuwaiti agreed to help Don smuggle in his friends. When he brought the first American to Don's apartment, however, he was followed. All three were captured. The soldiers beat the Kuwaiti, trying to get from him the names of others involved in the plot. He refused to answer and was shot as the two Americans were taken away.

"He gave his life rather than reveal my name," Mark grieved, when he heard it. "What loyalty! And I didn't even know the fellow."

Violence struck close by when troops searched a Kuwaiti house two doors from the church and found a Britisher. Guards brought him out to stand in the street. Then they rounded up the family of five—the youngest a child of six and the oldest a grandmother. Without warning they shot all five, leaving them where they fell. The Britisher they marched away.

Late that night Mark and two other Westerners hiding nearby retrieved the bodies and wrapped them in sheets for burial. The Resistance picked them up.

"Greater love hath no man than this—that a man lay down his life for his friends." That verse came to have a new and powerful meaning in the context of the Kuwait conflict.

About this time, Del received a letter from Mark. His account of the day's activities made her both laugh and cry.

I got a call from our Indian friend, Sadiq, last Friday. "I think I have a plan to get you out with the Indian convoy," he said. "Do you want to go?"

His proposal caught me by surprise, as such a thing was the furthest from my mind! After thinking for a long split second and considering all the subtleties of his proposition, I blurted out an instant *Yes!*

His letter went on to tell her that he'd been sunbathing each day on the rooftop, now that the weather was cooler, and had found that his hair was turning blond. Using some old lemons from the refrigerator, he aided the bleaching process, finally reaching a hair shade that he felt was fairly attractive. Now Sadiq was suggesting that he disguise himself as an Indian—and Indians have black hair!

I managed to get hold of some black dye. I tried to dye my hair, but in the process, got it on my face. It wouldn't wash off. I decided that wasn't such a bad idea—I'd dye my skin too. So I poured it on my hands and rubbed it all over my face, neck, arms, and legs. The rubber gloves that came with the dye made smear streaks on my skin, so I pitched them and used my bare hands. I thought I was doing a pretty good job until I saw my naked self in the mirror. I looked like an Oreo cookie! Black on the top and bottom, and white in the middle, where I'd run out of dye! How I laughed!

Then I caught sight of my hands. The palms were jet black. By repeatedly pouring the dye into my hands, I'd dyed my palms darkest of all. Since Indians have light-colored palms, I didn't think I could palm that off on any Iraqi guard!

So I started trying to lighten it up. I tried your nail-polish remover, then lacquer thinner, Brillo pads, Dettol toilet cleaner, pumice stone, and finally, straight Clorox and steel wool! That was a raw deal! With a lot of elbow grease, I finally got my palms a few shades lighter. But when I looked at my face and arms again, the dye seemed splotchy. I didn't dare go out like that.

That night on the phone I was telling one of our friends about the dilemma I was in. He said his wife had some henna dye I could use. I was sure that henna had a reddish tinge, and I told him so. "I don't want to go out as a *red* Indian!" I told him.

He said, "No, it won't turn red. Just mix it with some vinegar and a touch of toilet cleaner, and it will turn your skin black."

"With the toilet cleaner, are you sure I won't just look *flushed*?" I asked him.

Anyway, he got me the henna. I mixed the brew and took the plunge, trying it on the inside of one arm. I turned red.

So I called the Resistance and asked if they could get me more black dye. A courier brought me two bottles the next day, and I started over again.

By now my skin was reacting differently because of the first layer of dye. This time, I mixed the dye in three batches because I'd noted that after it set awhile, it changed color. So I reasoned that if I mixed each batch fresh and used one for each area of my body, I wouldn't run short, and the color would be the same. I wasn't able to get really accurate measurements on the batches, however, and each one was a slightly different shade. As a result, I turned out a tri-colored Indian!

I ended up trying to blend my face with candle soot. It looked OK in the apartment, but out in the light it looked awful. Unless I was traveling with a bunch of Indian clowns all similarly painted, I didn't know how I'd get through.

Mark figured the dye should last about ten days, time enough to exit the country if he didn't bathe. Meanwhile, the dye was coming off on his sheets, towels, and shirts. The first Indian convoy of seventy buses was leaving the next day, the Friday before Thanksgiving. He planned to be on one of them.

Then the Resistance called.

"Don't go with that group on Friday," they warned. "There's a rumor that an American plans to go with the Indians, and the Iraqis will be looking for him."

Mark's heart sank. He decided to drop the whole thing. But Sadiq urged him to go with him on Sunday instead. A ten-bus convoy was leaving then, going straight to Jordan, not stopping in Baghdad. It sounded good.

Sunday morning Sadiq took him to the school where the evacuation buses were assembled. This was the first time Mark had been away from the house since he had gone into hiding.

Sadiq stopped at a military checkpoint and spoke to the soldier. The guard waved them on, but Mark was sweating. In the bright desert sun, he thought the dye looked more splotchy than ever.

They negotiated another checkpoint successfully, but the farther they got from the apartment, the more uneasy Mark became. Finally he could stand it no longer.

"Take me back, Sadiq," he begged. "I can't go through with this. If I'm captured as an Indian, I may be shot. If they find out I'm an American, all of *you* may be shot, or I may be killed as a spy. I don't know why I ever thought this would work."

Ignoring his own danger, Sadiq drove back through the checkpoints to deliver the American safely home. Mark was greatly relieved. The risk to himself was too great. The risk to others was too great. And the risk that he would not see his family again was one Mark didn't even want to think about!

Soon after he got back to the apartment, the phone rang. It was a stranger calling from the Holiday Inn to inform Mark that he had a message for him from friends at Pacific Union College and would be by to deliver it in a few hours. Mark was instantly suspicious.

Calling the Resistance hotline, he explained the situation.

"Can you have a contact at the hotel check this guy out?" he pleaded.

"How will we know if he's legit?" they asked.

Mark thought fast and prayed hard. If he really was

from Pacific Union College, what might the man have that would identify him?

"Uh—I think he might have a college medallion on his key chain," he guessed.

"We'll see what we can do," the contact replied and hung up.

Mark paced the apartment, wondering whether to retreat to the cave. An hour later, two men turned up at the door, one of them a Resistance member who Mark knew. He invited them in.

"Mark, this is Kevin Brown, a special agent for the Chiquita Banana Company. He was sitting at the hotel phone table with his keys in front of him when I walked in. And sure enough, he had a college medallion on his key ring. So I spoke to him. He wants to help you escape."

Mark could hardly believe his ears. In the discussion that followed, he learned that Kevin had been hired by the Chiquita Company to find Ron and get him out of Kuwait. After Ron escaped, he suggested to his bosses that they try to get Mark out, stressing how the Adventist pastor had provided shelter and food for him during the previous six weeks. The company agreed.

During a flight from Jordan to Washington, Kevin had begun talking to the passenger next to him, finally revealing that he had been on an assignment to find a businessman hiding with an Adventist pastor in Kuwait. The businessman had recently been freed, however, and the agent was now concerned about the pastor.

Startled, his seatmate sat bolt upright.

"I can't believe this! I'm an Adventist! We've all been concerned about Mark Enden in Kuwait. I'll bet your businessman was staying with him. I can tell you where the church is, and Mark lives in the apartment right above it!"

Now it was Kevin's turn to look astonished. During the rest of the flight, the Adventist gave Kevin a phone number, a crude map, and a way of identifying himself.

"Say you come from Pacific Union College," he urged. "Here. Take my medallion to prove it. That should convince him to talk to you."

So here he was. The church headquarters had sent with him letters for Mark, a gas mask, an antidote for chemical warfare, and $5,000 in cash. Del had sent a letter and a picture of herself and the boys. Pangs of homesickness swept over Mark as he saw the familiar faces. Ryan looked so mischievous tickling Baby Loren. With difficulty, Mark forced himself to concentrate on what his visitor was saying.

"Everyone is anxious to help you get out," Kevin told Mark. "Not only is your church headquarters working on it, but someone from Chiquita calls your wife every day and gives her updates on the situation. They're paying all of Del's long-distance phone calls, and she's made a lot of them lately between trying to get you released and keeping your relatives informed. They're scattered from Pakistan to the Cayman Islands, you know!

"The fruit company has top-notch people who specialize in this sort of thing, and they've set up a round-the-clock 'situation room' at company headquarters. I've been trying to get into Kuwait for several weeks—and finally made it. We had hoped to have you out by Thanksgiving, but since that's too close now, how about Christmas?"

Mark was so overwhelmed that he had difficulty saying anything. He'd expected that the church would try to help him but not a company he didn't know. He promised himself that he'd buy only Chiquita bananas for the rest of his life!

After explaining a possible rescue plan, Kevin left quickly. Not staying in one place very long was part of his technique. He left Kuwait that day and continued working on Mark's escape from outside the country.

Del's letter told more about what the church headquarters was doing to obtain his release.

"Elder Battle and Elder Mittleider have been working on it night and day," she wrote. "They're in touch with the State Department constantly and with other governments that might help you. I think we'll have you out of there soon."

Later that night two Indian friends who had decided to remain in Kuwait came to cheer him up. They assumed that he would be discouraged after the convoy had left without him and were surprised to find him fairly cheerful already. They brought with them an Uno game, a ping-pong ball, and paddles. As they leaped back and forth after the ball, laughing and joking, tensions melted, and Mark began to relax.

In the small hours of the morning after they had gone, Mark sat on the rooftop, watching the stars twinkle over the desert. So much had happened that day! He'd tried to leave with Sadiq and returned home just in time to receive Kevin's call. His choice of a college medallion as a proof of authenticity must have been an idea from the Lord. And it was certainly no accident that Kevin sat by an Adventist on that flight! For that matter, it was no accident that Ron had been quartered with him rather than with some other American. Having a glimpse of God's behind-the-scenes working left him in awe. What a terrific God he served! And He used any means to accomplish His ends—the church, the State Department, and even the Chiquita Banana Company!

Chapter 10

Between Hope and Despair

With no one to share the apartment, time dragged. Mark thought of starting a diary, but he felt he just couldn't deal with writing out his emotions. If they were in his head, he could sometimes ignore them. On paper, they became real.

The Iraqis announced a reward for every Westerner betrayed. For the first time, Mark truly faced the reality that everything of value to him, including his life, could be lost. He smuggled out a letter to Del through friends of a friend of a friend. In it he poured out his feelings.

When Kevin brought me that picture of you and the boys, I nearly cried. I felt overwhelmed by my love for the family. It's stronger than it's ever been before. If there's one thing I have to live for, it's you guys.

Thoughts of you brighten the moments of each long day. It is to this deep well that I frequently come to be refreshed and where I feel most secure. I remember and I hope, and somehow find the strength, the ability to endure this terrific loneliness and the crushing silence that surrounds me.

I long each day to be able to hold you in my arms and experience the assurance that we are together once again. I cannot see beyond the veil of time, and fears of uncertainty hauntingly lurk in the shadows of my mind, threatening to crumble the fragile façade I am trying to maintain. What sustains me is our love and the commitment we have to each other. My love for you is the deepest emotion I have ever had. My belief in your love is the reason for my being. I know that I have not said that enough, but from my heart, it is truth for me. I regret every lost opportunity to express my love to you, and if I have the chance to be with you in the future, I wonder if I will be able to open up and show how I truly feel, or if I will be afraid to show the depth of my emotions as before. I will work toward that goal.

The American kept a suitcase packed, always ready to leave at a moment's notice. He also packed a box of family pictures and treasures and stashed it in a closet. The strain began to tell on him.

He spent a lot of time praying and thinking. At one point the Lord showed Mark that he was praying almost exclusively for himself and his own safety and that he needed to put more time and effort into praying for others. When Mark did so, he felt less depressed.

Mark decided to occupy himself by trying to bake bread. It turned out so well that he made more, sharing it with others in hiding. Before long his bread baking became an elaborate ritual that he really enjoyed. He even made cinnamon rolls, filling them with raisins he had made himself by drying courtyard grapes on the roof.

"Del would be proud of me," he thought. "I'll have to bake her some bread when I get home."

At that point, Mark deliberately changed his train of thought. Thinking of Del and the boys easily got him down.

After his unsuccessful attempt to escape, Mark's Resistance contact delivered to him a Siamese kitten. It had belonged to a British electronics expert who had rigged his apartment with cameras and security devices to protect himself. In spite of these precautions, he was captured. He had even been working on a satellite phone link so those in hiding could get messages out of Kuwait. His captors hustled him off to Baghdad, and his kitten wound up with Mark.

"His name is Saddam Hussein," someone told Mark.

"Maybe—but I'm going to call him Bashim!" Mark announced. "That's a good Pakistani name!"

The little ball of fur really helped to fill the empty apartment. Mark spent hours playing with the kitten. It slept on his bed, sat on his lap whenever he sat down, and howled if he walked out of the room. Mark was amazed at how much company the tiny creature was and thanked the Lord for sending it.

He was also grateful for the antenna booster he had received from the kitten's former owner. During the summer, it had been impossible to get CNN news from Bahrain or Dubai, but as the humidity increased, it formed a dome over the Gulf area and bounced the signals to Kuwait more frequently. The electronic device boosted the power on his TV antenna, and Mark began receiving CNN news regularly, a great relief after all the Baghdad propaganda.

A daring woman who was a member of the Resistance stopped by one day to leave some money and fresh vegetables. She stayed a few minutes to chat with Mark, giving him the latest news and leaving with him the humorous little underground news sheet. That night he was horrified to hear that she had been captured during the day. Finding so much money on her, the soldiers assumed correctly that she was connected with the Resistance. Enraged, they not only killed her, but cut her body into pieces, which they left at the front door of her family home. All over Kuwait, people in hiding mourned the death of this brave patriot.

Mark was tempted to hate the killers, but in his heart he knew that the cruel atrocities were carried out by relatively few. Most of the soldiers on both sides were decent fellows like himself, caught in a war that was none of their making, longing to be back home. Many had been kind to him and others in hiding. He knew, too, that some residents of the city were taking advantage of the situation to loot and kill for their own gain. This all had more to do with evil and human nature than with national origins.

The week of Thanksgiving, a group of British men hiding a few doors down the street from the church called to suggest he come and spend the holiday with them. It wasn't a British holiday, of course, but they felt sorry for the American who was alone on a family-oriented occasion. Since his skin was still dyed, Mark decided to disguise himself as a Kuwaiti and go.

Because the possibility of capture had been weighing heavily on his mind, he called a Kuwaiti friend and asked him whether he could store a few precious items for him, along with Luisa's car and Mark's Mitsubishi, which he was already hiding. The man agreed to pick up the things sometime during the next few days. Mark carefully packed a large briefcase with the church funds and valuable documents and set it by the desk, ready to give him.

On Wednesday night, he put on a Kuwaiti robe and flowing headdress and took with him his passport, the $5,000 the church had sent him, and his small shortwave radio. He also took some fresh rolls he had baked to add to the Thanksgiving dinner. Shortly before midnight, he strolled down the street to his friends' house, knocking at their door with a coded rap. They welcomed him in, talked awhile, and then showed him where to sleep—and where to hide, in case of a raid. Everyone had assigned hiding places.

Thanksgiving morning shots rang out in the street. A gunfight had broken out in front of the church. After peering through the curtains for a few minutes and watching sand fly as the bullets bit the street, Mark and his friends disappeared into their hiding places. The usual Iraqi response to such gunfights was to seal off the area and start a house-to-house search for Resistance fighters. For two hours the men hid, not knowing what was happening. Finally, when all seemed quiet, they emerged and began fixing Thanksgiving dinner.

Being with friends again felt wonderful. Mark reveled in the talk and laughter, trying to store up some of it as a buffer against later loneliness. When dinner was on the table, he could hardly believe his eyes! Broccoli and cauliflower! Potatoes and pumpkin pie! His hosts had even found a frozen turkey, having no idea that he preferred a vegetarian diet. That day, however, he ate turkey and found it delicious.

The holiday passed all too quickly. Mark stayed until nearly midnight before venturing out for the walk home. Thanking his friends for a wonderful holiday, he made his way cautiously back to the church. At the front door, he stood frozen with terror. The door was open. All was dark inside, but in the dim light, he could see several items in the sanctuary were out of place.

He stood in the doorway, heart pounding, straining to hear any movement upstairs. After a long minute of complete silence, he slipped inside and closed the door. Stealthily he climbed the stairs, dreading what he might find.

As he switched on the apartment light, he saw immediately that the TV was missing. The Xerox machine, the church's VCR, the sound equipment—all were gone. Ironically, the thieves had stolen the large shortwave radio that sat beside the computer but left the more expensive computer there.

"They probably didn't know what to do with it," Mark guessed.

The intruders had rifled through drawers and suitcases,

selecting just the things they wanted. To his horror, he noticed that the packed briefcase was gone. Whoever had been in the apartment now had his ministerial license, his marriage license, and other documents that clearly identified him as an American. They also had all the church funds. Suddenly something bumped his ankles. He jumped and whirled around. To his relief, it was only the kitten, welcoming him home.

Scooping it up, Mark ran to the bedroom and grabbed a sports bag with a shoulder strap. Into it he jammed a shirt and a pair of pants, underclothes and shaving gear. As he passed the hall closet, he noted that the box of family photos was still there. In the living room, he snatched up his Bible, *The Desire of Ages*, and *Steps to Christ*—the books that had meant the most to him. He also grabbed the box of computer disks containing the names and addresses of the Gulf members and pushed them into the big pocket of his Kuwaiti robe, where the small shortwave radio already lay hidden.

At the last minute, he disconnected the telephone and crammed it into the bag, too, tugging at the zipper to get it closed. He flung the bag onto his shoulder, cradled Bashim in the other arm, and looked around one last time. There were still many valuable things in the apartment. Some had cash value; others had sentimental value. But nothing was too valuable to leave when his life was on the line.

Turning out the lights and closing the door, he made his way back to the British home by a long and devious route, checking behind him every few minutes to be sure he wasn't being followed. At his destination, he rapped with the coded signal. The door swung open, and a startled Englishman pulled him inside.

"What on earth happened?" he asked. "You look awful!"

Over a hot drink, Mark told them what he had found. Their sympathy and caring eased his pain. Just having someone to talk to helped. His fears had been realized.

Most of his possessions were gone. Still, he had his passport, radio, money, his life—and Bashim.

"What luck that you were here with us!" his host exclaimed. "That gun battle in the street attracted the soldiers, and while they were checking out your place, they found they'd stumbled onto a hideout. If you'd been home, you'd have been captured for sure!"

"That wasn't luck," Mark told them. "I've been away from the apartment only once before tonight. I think the Lord got me out of there just in the nick of time."

The next day the Resistance relocated him in an apartment across the street from an Iraqi post in another part of the city. The apartment had been left vacant by an Italian couple who had fled earlier.

"Do you think this apartment is safe?" he asked the Resistance contact anxiously. "I'm so close to Iraqi headquarters."

The man laughed.

"That's what makes it so safe," he chuckled. "This building has been cleared already. The Westerners who are still living here are doing so with permission. There's a European man in an apartment below you. He was arrested with a friend and slated to go to Baghdad as a human shield, but he argued with the officials, proving Hungarian citizenship, and they let him go. He's a writer. He'll be your contact. Only he and I know you are here."

So Mark began living in a furnished apartment someone else had abandoned. To his delight, the man's clothing hanging in the closets fit him, and the fellow had excellent taste too. When it came to reading, however, the Italian books stumped him!

Locating a telephone jack and plugging in his phone, Mark dialed the group of British men to let them know he was safe.

"What's your number, pal?" one asked. "We'll give you a ring now and then."

Mark began to laugh uncontrollably.

"I don't know what my number is," he gasped, trying to catch his breath, "and there's no way to find out without revealing that I'm here. I can call out, but no one can call in! This is so funny!"

His friends laughed with him, but there was no solution to the problem without contacting authorities to get the phone number. At least he could call out.

One of Mark's first calls was to the Kuwaiti friend who had planned to hide the church funds for him. "When it's safe, would you go over to my apartment and get that box of photos and family things in the hall closet? And take the computer too. Keep them till I'm free, and I'll be in touch with you to get them back. Can you do that?"

"Inshah Allah!" the man responded. "God willing!"

The next day the Kuwaiti reported that the items were safely in his possession. Mark felt he had much to be thankful for. He wrote a letter to Del, hoping to smuggle it to her somehow.

I've almost given up the idea of a soon release. The pendulum of hope swings back and forth. It's exhausting. And I keep listening for another message from you on Voice of America. I notice that some people talk for several minutes, and others are on repeatedly. Those of us who are stuck here don't appreciate the partiality! Get after those guys to let you talk to me.

Bashim prowled around the apartment, sniffing at his new home. Soon the Hungarian man from downstairs came up to introduce himself, and in the days that followed, he stopped by the apartment nearly every day to talk for an hour or two. He fell in love with Bashim instantly.

"I had a cat too," Jozsef told Mark, stroking the kitten. "I left it in front of the apartment when they arrested me, and I don't know what happened to it. It's nice to have one sharpening its claws on my leg again."

During their lengthy discussions, the two men explored a wide variety of topics. To his delight, Jozsef discovered that Mark used the same bread recipe he did—one that had come from a health-reconditioning center in Maine! The fact that they both had visited this institution and were interested in healthful living seemed to cement their friendship.

From his window, Mark could look down on the building next door. Military trucks backed up to the house regularly, unloading large canisters.

"What are they storing next door?" he asked Jozsef.

"Cylinders of gas for chemical warfare," the man replied grimly. "I pray God stops them before they can use it. Oh, by the way, your friend Kevin contacted the Resistance this week. He said they're still working on getting you out."

That was encouraging, but with the gas next door, Mark wished he had the gas mask and the chemical antidote he had left in the apartment. On second thought, maybe he didn't leave them. Perhaps they had been stolen. He hadn't noticed. At any rate, they were gone, and he decided he'd just have to trust the Lord on that one. He'd come through very well so far.

Locked in the apartment day after day, Mark had a lot of time to think. This experience was changing his priorities. During the past few months, he had begun to realize that there are very few things a person can't get along without. He promised himself that if he were freed, he would make more time for God, family, personal growth, and artistic development. When the chips were down, these were the things that mattered. Everything else could be replaced or eliminated.

He had come to Kuwait to minister to others. The Lord had led him into a different type of ministry than he had ever imagined, but looking back at it, Mark felt it was definitely a ministry. Reassuring others, caring for their safety, talking about the vital issues of life—all these had been part of his ministry. Maybe the Lord had something to teach him, too, about the preciousness of his sons and his wife. In the past he had often taken them for granted. God helping him, he resolved to change that if he got out of Kuwait.

On Thursday, December 6, Kuwait radio announced that all Westerners would be allowed to leave. Saddam Hussein had guaranteed them safe passage out of the country. Either the soldiers didn't hear it, or the announcement was a hoax, for they continued rounding up hostages that day and the next.

Mark and most other Westerners in hiding viewed the announcement with suspicion. After all, the same man who said he wouldn't invade Kuwait was now promising them safe passage out of it! The embassy advised them to keep a low profile.

Friday, Mark spent much time pacing, making phone calls, and listening to the Voice of America. Suddenly he heard Del.

"The kids and I are fine," she told him. "The boys have bronchitis, but they'll get over it. I've had two wisdom teeth removed, and Loren is still teething like crazy. Keep up your courage! Things are moving fast now. Watch for the big Dutchman. He will say, 'I am the big Dutchman.' He will help you."

Mark's heart pounded as he heard Del's voice. "Oh, God, help me get back to her and the kids," he prayed. "Whether the big Dutchman gets me out, or we are released, just help me get home."

Word on the American underground was that the ambassador was trying to get written assurances and guarantees for their safety. The young man had a hard time sleeping Friday night.

Sabbath dawned bright and hot. The network had nothing new to report except that soldiers were still rounding up hostages in some areas. Finally, late Saturday afternoon, Voice of America and the BBC announced that all Westerners could now emerge from hiding. Jozsef came running upstairs to tell him that the American ambassador had obtained seats for his citizens on Iraqi planes departing on Sunday.

Mark found a suitcase in the closet and packed some of the clothes he'd been wearing. Then, running down to Jozsef's apartment, he banged on the door. "I'm free!" he shouted. "I'm going outside!"

On the street he stopped to look around. Westerners were emerging from one building after another. Twenty or thirty Iraqi soldiers who had been lounging on the lawn across the street stared in amazement at all the foreigners coming from houses right under their noses. For a moment, the air was tense.

Then, all at once, a soldier began clapping. Others joined him, and they started shouting to the foreigners in both English and Arabic.

"Congratulations!" they yelled. "Hooray for you!" "Congratulations on your freedom!"

Mark walked over to them, talking and joking, with a marvelous sense of freedom. Then he joined the other Americans and walked on down the street.

That Saturday night the Westerners had one long party. Piling into cars, they moved from place to place, hugging, kissing, singing, and shouting in celebration of their freedom. At last all the phone voices took on faces. Mark hugged people he'd only talked to before, thanking them for their encouragement and exchanging addresses for future contacts.

Early in the morning he came back to the apartment, collected his suitcase, and made his way to Jozsef's door. The Hungarian had no plans to leave Kuwait and had agreed to drive him to the airport.

"I'm out of here," Mark announced. "But since you plan

to stay in the country, would you like Bashim?"

Jozsef's eyes lighted up as he reached for the kitten.

"Of course!" he exclaimed. "I'll miss you, Mark, but I'd love to have the kitten. Thank you for all our talks and your friendship. Maybe we meet again someday, huh?"

Mark picked up his suitcase.

"I hope so," he joked, "but I hope the conditions are better. We've really been between Iraq and a hard place here!"

Laughing merrily, Jozsef followed him out to the car.

Chapter 11
Flight to Freedom

Kuwait City was strangely quiet as they drove to the civilian airport that Sunday. No sounds of bombs, tanks, or antiaircraft guns broke the early-morning stillness. Once-magnificent buildings now displayed holes like gaping wounds. Street lights and traffic lights were missing. Burned tanks, trucks, and cars cluttered the streets, and the smell of burning rubber still hung in the air. A beautiful and luxurious city lay devastated.

At the civilian airport, the Westerners found buses waiting. "All luggage on this bus," an Iraqi official shouted. And the men put their suitcases into that bus. As they boarded the passenger buses, the luggage bus pulled out ahead and sped out of sight. The men looked at one another suspiciously. Where had the luggage gone?

The buses carried them to the military airport. The luggage was not there. The men began to complain. "You took our luggage an hour ago. Where is it?"

"We want our suitcases back. Somebody may be going through them."

"We're getting out of here with little enough as it is. We need those suitcases."

After an absence of an hour and a half, the bus returned.

111

The Americans were clearly upset.

"Maybe someone planted bombs in our luggage," one suggested. "That would ensure that we don't get away alive."

"Let's check our stuff," another agreed. "Everybody find his own luggage and go through it carefully. Be sure nothing has been taken or added."

So the men retrieved their bags and began going through them methodically. Their suspicions were well-founded—someone *had* been through many of the bags, including Mark's. But nothing seemed to have been added or stolen. Closing the bags again, they loaded them into the Iraqi Air 707 jets that waited on the runway.

The men looked at the aircraft skeptically too. The planes were old and the maintenance, doubtful. The luggage bin over Mark's head wouldn't stay closed, so it hung open the entire trip. Seats wouldn't work, and lights were defective.

"You know, it's international law that these airline pilots log a certain amount of time in the air each month to stay licensed," Mark's seatmate muttered to him. "I'll bet these guys are flying illegally because with the restrictions, they probably haven't been able to get their planes into the air at all."

"This whole scenario is not reassuring," Mark agreed.

The jets, which were to have left at 9:00 a.m., finally took off for Baghdad at 2:30 that afternoon. Mark's plane banked sharply to avoid Saudi airspace and headed north. Inside the aircraft, the atmosphere was tense. No one had had lunch. They were still in Iraqi hands, flying in Iraqi planes. Was it all a hoax? The past five months of alternating hope and despair kept many of them from rejoicing in their freedom just yet. They wouldn't believe it completely until they were beyond their captors' control.

As if to reinforce those fears, when the plane landed in Baghdad, it was detained.

"What on earth is going on?" Mark asked an attendant. "Why aren't we leaving?"

The man shrugged. "Sorry, sir. The officials in charge of getting clearance to travel through Turkish airspace forgot to get permission for our flight. Last week three of our planes were forced down in Turkey and held for some time because they didn't have clearance. We don't want that to happen again, so we wait here for permission."

Tensions mounted as the hours passed. The passengers were finally allowed to go to the airport's duty-free shop. The only items for sale there were boxes of dates and bottles of liquor. Mark bought ten boxes of the delicious Middle Eastern dates to take to Del and the family. Many of the passengers bought liquor, took it back to the plane, and started drinking. To pass the time, they talked to one another, finding connections in their lives. Some of the Americans they picked up in Baghdad had been used as human shields and had interesting tales to tell. Others were part of the American embassy team in Baghdad.

"You fellows helped to get my wife and boys out, I think," Mark said. "I'm Mark Enden from Kuwait. Del Enden came through with the British contingent. Do you remember her?"

The men laughed. "How could we forget? We'd seen a lot of action, but those kids of yours topped it! They never ran down! We could see Del needed a break, so we took over for the morning. Pete here ran himself ragged retrieving the ball they threw out of the pool every twenty-eight seconds, and Gina hasn't gotten all the crayons out from under her nails yet! They were great kids! They really took our minds off the tension that day.

"By the way, tell her that the British schoolboy she was worried about did get caught at the airport and just yesterday was released from the military camp where they'd taken him. She seemed interested in his welfare."

Mark laughed. "That's my wife, all right! Thanks so much for helping her. Boy, is she going to be surprised when I call tonight!"

"If we ever leave here," muttered an engineer. "I wonder

if they really intend to let us go or not."

"I don't think we'll ever get out of here alive," one pessimist muttered after four hours. "Hussein's playing games with us. It's an old trick to wear the prisoners down. Give 'em hope and dash it!"

Mark refused to believe that. Silently he talked with God. "Please, Lord, don't let us get this far and get stopped," he begged. "You have the power to overrule. Get that clearance for us—please! Remember Your promise? Ask, and I'll receive? You *will* save me? Thank You so much for keeping me safe thus far. Thank You for the contacts I made and the chances I had to witness for You. If it's not Your will for us to be free, help me to handle it. But if it's Your will, please send that clearance through."

After five hours of tense waiting, clearance finally arrived, and the planes took off for Germany. During the flight, the Iraqi crew became more friendly and served a hot meal. Before long they were above Frankfurt. Then, once over the city, they circled and circled.

"What's wrong now?" Mark asked the attendant. "Why aren't we landing?"

"We can't lower the plane's flaps on one side," the attendant admitted. "The pilot is getting advice from the control tower."

Mark groaned. Would they never get out of this plane?

The control tower and the pilot finally decided to land the plane with only half of the flaps operable. Rescue vehicles stood by as the plane landed on the longest available runway. The pilot handled the plane well and brought it down safely at about 1:00 a.m. As they left the plane, the passengers broke into spontaneous shouting and singing. They were free at last.

Representatives from the American State Department gathered their citizens and loaded them onto buses for the short trip to the airport's Sheraton Hotel.

"Your rooms are waiting for you," the official announced.

"Pick up your keys at the desk. I assume most of you will want to make phone calls to assure your loved ones that you are safe now. Please feel free to do so. Your government will pick up the tab for all your long-distance calls, so enjoy yourselves. We are delighted that you are free!"

The travelers cheered and swarmed around the registration desk. As he lined up to get a room key, Mark felt overwhelmed with joy and thankfulness.

"Thank You, Lord," he prayed silently. "Thank You, thank You, thank You!"

As soon as keys were issued, everyone dashed off to his room to find a phone. Mark found out immediately that international calls couldn't be made from his room. Hurrying down to the lobby, he found long lines already formed in front of each public phone. He attached himself to the end of one and settled in for a lengthy wait.

When he finally got Del on the line, he could hardly speak. Later, he couldn't remember what they talked about, but the bill came to $350!

"All those taxes we paid are finally doing some good," Mark later told Del.

When he finished talking to her, he called Ron. "Call off the troops," Mark told him. "I'm in Frankfurt!"

"Way to go, man," shouted Ron. "Good for you. When will you be home? We want you to come to Ohio and see the Chiquita Company, you know. Everyone working on the case wants to meet you guys."

On his next call, he tried to contact his parents, who were then in Thailand, but never reached them. Exhausted, he headed upstairs for bed. He'd been running on nervous energy for three days. He needed sleep.

But when he got into the big bed, his mind kept racing. Part of him was exhausted from the tension and wanted to sleep. Another part of him could hardly be still. With similarly mixed emotions, he couldn't decided whether to laugh or cry.

"Probably all that adrenalin," he told himself and rose to take a long, hot shower. He grinned as he let the water run luxuriously down the drain. No need to save it for flushing the toilet now!

The next day, the State Department transported the group back to the airport, where they boarded Pan American jets for the final leg of their trip home.

The crew greeted them with unusual warmth. "Welcome back, fellows!" The flight attendant's American accent sounded wonderful. "As soon as we are airborne, we will be serving you all the French fries, soft drinks, and Big Macs you want, courtesy of McDonald's!"

The passengers cheered and laughed, everyone trying to talk at once. The mood of exhilaration continued throughout the entire flight, even though passengers did settle down long enough to organize a class-action suit against the Iraqi government.

"We are definitely a bunch of happy campers," Mark told his seatmate.

"You bet!" was the hearty response. "God bless America!"

The plane landed at Andrews Air Force Base in Washington, D.C. Del, her parents, and the boys had driven down from Reading and were eagerly waiting with Mark's two brothers for his arrival. Dozens of other families stood with them behind a high chain-link fence bordering the airfield. The jet stopped short of the terminal and waited while airport crews pushed a staircase up to the door. Buses waited close by.

The next two hours were among the most frustrating of the entire trip. While Mark usually waited for others to leave a plane and was among the last to disembark, this time he was the eighth person down the stairs. Behind the distant fence he could see people waving frantically. He waved back but never really recognized anyone. Officials urged passengers to board the bus quickly.

After a short ride, the travelers were herded into a large

conference room, where State Department officials held a debriefing, questioning the travelers for over an hour. While the officials were nice enough, they took up precious time. Everyone wanted to get to his family, but no family members were allowed in that area. With increasing impatience, the escapees told their versions of captivity and hiding.

"I don't think we're out of captivity yet," one quipped.

"Keep a low profile," another called out.

That brought a hearty laugh, and the returnees began chanting softly. "Keep a low profile! Keep a low profile!"

When they were finally allowed to enter the gymnasium, where their families waited with increasing impatience, it was one at a time. An official would call out the returnee's name over the loudspeaker, and his relatives would surge forward and claim him. When that reunion was over, another name was announced. It seemed like an endless process.

"Mark Enden!" the officer called. Mark picked up his bag and ran out the door. Family and friends of the previously released man blocked his way, and he saw no one he recognized. Suddenly he saw Del, pushing through the crowd toward him.

"Mark!" she shouted, and then she was in his arms, smothering him with kisses. Taking his free hand, she led him back through the crowd to the family. To his surprise, two of the men from the General Conference were there to welcome him, Kenneth Mittleider and Maurice Battle. Elder Battle was holding Loren.

"Welcome back," they told him. "We're certainly glad to see you. Everyone's been praying for you night and day."

Mark was having a hard time focusing on everyone at once. His two brothers, Bob and Steve, were thumping him on the back while Del's parents crowded forward to get hugs. To his astonishment, Luisa Lane appeared.

"What on earth are you doing here?" he sputtered. "I

thought you were in England!"

Luisa laughed. "You kept talking about America so much that I came over here to check it out! I'm working here in Washington now. Welcome home, stranger!"

The group faced two more delays. Their luggage had not arrived, and the news media descended on them, shouting questions and taking pictures. It was nine o'clock before they left the airport, four hours after the plane's arrival. None of the returnees had anticipated such long, drawn-out procedures at the airport.

As the family talked, they made their way to the cars. Mark looked at his sons with new eyes. "How they've grown during these five months," he thought. "How much I've missed! I must remember my priority list. More time for God and family."

After all the exhilaration, Mark was worn out even before the three-hour drive to Reading and thought he had no more emotion left. But as they neared the Joneses' home, an air of excitement rippled through the car. Mark wondered what it was all about until they drove up in front of the house. Ribbons, streamers, banners, balloons, and flags hung from every conceivable spot.

"WELCOME HOME, MARK! THANK GOD YOU'RE BACK!"

Looking at the house, Mark almost cried. It was wonderful!

"Who did all this?" he asked.

"The church folks and neighbors," Dr. Jones replied proudly. "They've all been praying for you, and they worked for hours to get this ready. But they didn't expect you'd arrive in the middle of the night!"

That night the Endens and Joneses thanked God fervently for Mark's release. Although he didn't know it, all across America and in foreign lands, many others gave thanks to the Lord, too, for they'd all been praying for Mark Enden.

Chapter 12

The Aftermath

After so many months of isolation, being in the spotlight twenty-four hours a day was almost too much of a psychological overload. At times Mark wanted to hide away, even from the family.

The day after he arrived in Pennsylvania, Mark made front-page news and did a radio interview. The phone rang steadily for the rest of the week. People he knew, people he'd heard of, and people he'd never met were calling to rejoice in his freedom. Mark was nearly drowned in the wave of love that poured over him.

"It's Suzy, our friend from Pennsylvania," Del reported. "Talk to her." Mark took the receiver.

"You don't know how glad I am you're home," Suzy bubbled. "I've burned candles for your safe return every day since August 2. Stan says he had to take out extra fire insurance for all these candles, and now he has to repaint the interior to cover up all the smoke! I just know the Lord heard our prayers!"

Mark shook his head. Such caring!

A Baptist Bible-study group in Florida let him know he'd been the object of their prayers. A Catholic woman Mark had never met said her entire diocese had been saying novenas for his safe return. An Adventist church in Florida called to say the schoolchildren had been praying for him. Christians all across America had been praying. From near and far came messages of love and rejoicing.

Ron called from Ohio. "When the holidays are over, and you get time, the company would like you to stop by here and meet the people who were working on our release," Ron told him. "We want you to see the situation room and all that. We'll put you up. Just come."

"I can't get over this, Del," Mark confessed. "I've never felt such an outpouring of love—both from Adventists and non-Adventists! It must be the way heaven will be."

The Christmas that followed, according to Del, was the best ever. She had what she wanted for Christmas! Her husband!

After the holidays, the family drove to Tennessee to visit two of Mark's sisters, and on the way back, stopped in Cincinnati, Ohio, where they were housed in the elegant Garfield House, courtesy of the Chiquita Banana Company.

Ron took them home to meet his wife Kate and his baby daughter, Sarah. Mark was proud to introduce Del and the boys to his former housemate. In Ron's hospitable home they enjoyed a delicious meal and reminisced about their days in hiding. The next evening the two families went out for Indian food.

"You've corrupted me," Ron laughed. "All that rice and curry you fixed—I got to liking the stuff!"

At the Chiquita Company, the Endens visited the situation room and met all the people who had been working on getting Ron and Mark released.

That noon a special luncheon was held for the Endens on the top floor of the Chiquita building. The president, vice-president, legal counselors, Ron, and many others came to eat and talk with Mark and Del.

"I can't thank you enough for trying to save my life and for supporting Del the way you did," Mark told them. "You went far beyond the call of duty, and when I was most discouraged, I'd think of you and the church working to get me out, and I'd have hope again. God bless you!"

When the Endens arrived back in Pennsylvania, a big box was awaiting them. Inside they found Chiquita banana shirts, souvenirs, and giant blow-up swim bananas for the boys!

A few weeks later, Ron called to say he was coming to Pennsylvania on business and would drive down to see them. When he entered the house, he handed Mark a set of keys.

"You could use a car," he said, "and I want you to have my Saab. You have no idea how much I appreciate your taking me in like you did."

Mark and Del could hardly believe their eyes. A Saab? For them? But it was true. Ron had a plane ticket in his pocket for his trip back home.

"Thank You, Lord," Mark prayed that night. "What a bonus! We lost all our things—but we may get back that box of pictures, at least. The other things are replaceable. And the insurance money covered a lot. I can't replace my notes and some of my books, but maybe I needed some new ideas and new thoughts. All I can say is Praise the Lord!"

When the war broke out, Mark and Del watched the news avidly, commenting on the pictures.

"That picture's taken out by the airport!"

"The Entertainment Park is a total ruin!"

"Look what a mess they made of the beach!"

"Oh, no! The oil wells are on fire! What a tremendous waste."

As soon as the war was over, the church sent Mark to Iraq. This time he assisted in distributing food and medicine to the displaced Kurdish refugees. The sights he saw that May haunted him. Even when he returned to the States, he could still feel the tiny babies who died in his arms for lack of proper sanitation and medical care.

"Where do we go next?" he asked when he returned to the General Conference. "Back to Kuwait?"

"Not this year," he was told. "The country is in much worse condition than when you left it, and most of the church members are still in their homelands. We'll send you to another Middle Eastern country as soon as we make proper arrangements. Meanwhile, continue language study while you're here in Washington."

For the next six weeks Mark studied ten to twelve hours a day while Del bought and packed supplies for their next assignment. In July 1991, the Endens departed for a new post, where they will study the language and culture of the region while looking for opportunities to be of service to the people there.

"Aren't you afraid to go back to the Middle East?" a concerned friend asked them. "What if you get caught again?"

Del and Mark smiled.

"The Lord took care of us last time," Del reminded him. "What makes you think we can't trust Him again?"

"Besides," Mark added, "after that last assignment, we can't wait to see what God has in store for us next!"